★ *Duke* ★

IN HIS OWN WORDS

**JOHN WAYNE'S LIFE IN LETTERS,
HANDWRITTEN NOTES AND
NEVER-BEFORE-SEEN PHOTOS**

Contents

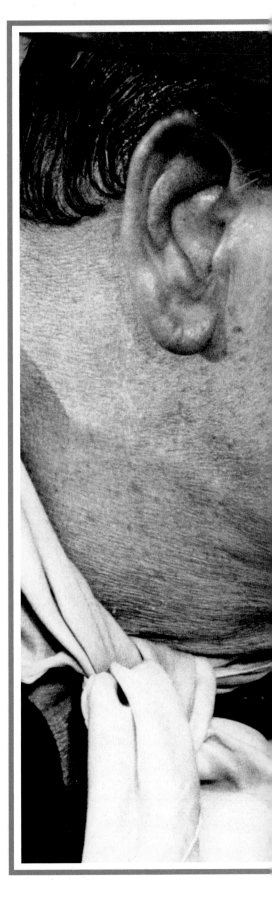

There's more to my father than meets the eye.

The entire world recognizes John Wayne as the iconic actor whose image is synonymous with American strength, kindness and dignity. But he once said, "The guy you see on the screen isn't really me. I'm Duke Morrison, and I never was and never will be a film personality like John Wayne. I know him well. I'm one of his closest students. I have to be. I make a living out of him." The truth is, the on-screen persona people loved only scratched the surface of who my father was. He wasn't John Wayne—he was better. And to discover the soul of the man who inspired the character, you need to dig deeper and look beyond the marquee. John Wayne spent hours poring over letters from family, friends and fans who wanted to connect with the man who meant so much to their lives. And every day, my father never failed to respond in kind, putting pen to paper and sharing his thoughts with the world. It didn't matter if the recipient was one of his kids, an admiring fan or the Commander in Chief. John Wayne always called it like he saw it, and the straightforward honesty the world glimpsed on the big screen reached new depths when he put his pen to paper. We've opened up the family archives to share stacks of my father's letters, telegrams and memos with the world because there is no better way to show his fans who that man was in real life: unguarded, unedited and always game for a good laugh.

Let us introduce you.

—ETHAN WAYNE

Analyzing Duke's
Penmanship

Annette Poizner, graphologist and psychotherapist, reveals what John Wayne's handwriting says about him.

THE WRITE STUFF

Annette Poizner is a Columbia-trained clinical social worker and is the author of *Clinical Graphology: An Interpretive Manual for Mental Health Practitioners.*

THE LETTER

This sample was pulled from the handwritten draft of Duke's *Variety* essay about the film industry, on page 156.

TEXTBOOK STYLE

"His handwriting presents us with a very interesting paradox. On one hand, the letters are fairly conservative, close to the copybook script that he would have learned in school. When a writer retains a handwriting style that beckons back to the one learned in his early years, graphologists find conservative tendencies and loyalties to more classic value systems. In this case we find a very conservative writing style, but at the same time the writer obviously deviates from handwriting norms by having irregular margins, making letters and words illegible and improperly using the written lines on the page."

A LITTLE MORE ACTION

"He often skips fully writing out words or roughly shapes letters in the rush to move on to the next word. We see a writer who was strongly movement-oriented—a man of action. The written line flies across the page as if the pen (and the person) cannot sit still. This is somebody who learned by doing. He loved variety, excitement, motion, taking risks."

THE GIVING GENE

"There is a wonderful graphic feature in this sample which is quite prominent. Duke slashes long T-bars, crossing the stems in a way that has him sweeping across the page. Classically, graphologists described that particular graphic trait as denoting a writer who is extremely generous, as if he routinely would send his life force outward to the left margin, the world of the other, to put himself out there, to be helpful and generous."

give us the right to
be *careless* ~~everywhere~~ *is ~~mould~~ in*
our results. Our art
is panorama of life the
salt and pepper the good
and the bad the oil
and the water the research
and its unreasonable *antagonism*
of human beings. There is
plenty of room for challenge
~~may~~ ~~Intel~~ and ~~hard~~
~~work~~ to produce positive
product. Negative thinking —
drawing away from one's
disparaging belittling
easier to degrade less
imagination to destroy a feeling
of hope than to build one
So if one would
make a *quick* buck
or become an *overnite*
personality the easiest
way is to tear down
the images destroy the
hopes and wishes of the
audience. Recently a long

PUSHING THE ENVELOPE

"This writer delighted in dynamism—in bold movement. He liked to push boundaries. He actually does push the boundaries of the page. Look at the word 'challenge' on this line. He is practically bumping into the right margin and shows that it's not past him to push the envelope, to take things a little too far, to ignore social conventions and keep pushing, keep thrusting, keep doing his thing."

CORRESPONDENCE CASANOVA

"Looking at this writing, you see a writer who just wants to keep moving the pen. He is unpredictable. Also, note that his lower zones (the huge sweeping loops in the lower part of the g, for example) indicate a sensuality that would promote a hunger for excitement and fun but also would contribute to skills in mechanical areas, working in a trade and working with his hands. Further, this writing shows a phenomenon we call 'crashing.' The lower zone of one line intermingles with the middle zone of the line below. The writer who intermingles those two zones shows subjectivity and a rich imagination, including a tendency to fantasize."

BELOVED FATHER
John Wayne joins in on playtime with his children Michael and Toni. Duke had a total of seven children, with an age gap of more than 30 years between his eldest, Michael, and his youngest, Marisa.

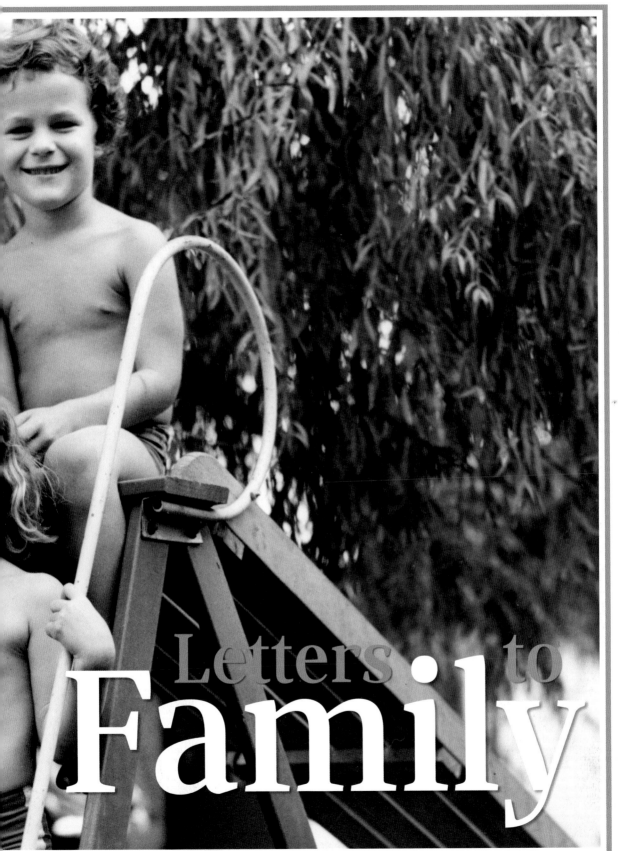

Letters to
Family

DUKE WITH HIS
YOUNGEST SON, ETHAN

 O MATTER HOW BUSY HIS SCHEDULE, JOHN WAYNE always kept in touch with loved ones, making time to share advice and laughs with his children, specifically. Most of the exchanges between Duke and his kin are short, simple and follow a basic theme—he was proud to be their dad. From an undated, handwritten letter in the 1960s to his daughter, Aissa, in which he thanks her for "making me a proud and happy father" to a moving April 1979 letter to his second oldest son, Patrick, written just weeks before his death, in which Duke wrote simply "my number two son is always a delight to me," John Wayne was eager to convey his pride in his children.

And they were similarly proud of him. Duke, in fact, was a towering presence in the lives of his children—Michael, Patrick, Toni and Melinda from his first marriage to Josephine Saenz, and Aissa, Ethan and Marisa from his third marriage to Pilar Pallete.

"He was just a regular dad," Melinda says. "He had a wonderful sense of humor but was adamant about school and always said that education was the key to life. He was very interested in our behavior and expected us to get good grades." These heartfelt sentiments jump off the letters on the pages to come.

"I am a demonstrative man, a baby picker-upper, a hugger and a kisser—that's my nature."

JOHN WAYNE WITH
GRANDSON MATTHEW MUÑOZ

February 15

Dear Daddy

Happy Valentines day. I hope you find Mexico more pleasant than Durango and that all the work goes smoothly down there for you.

I've really been upset since I broke off my engagement to Peggy I haven't been making much sense to anybody and very little more to myself. I've been doing a lot of thinking about it trying to figure out what I'm going to do. I've thought more about Marraige in the last 4 months than I ever have before. I've thought about peggy and how much I love her I've thought about marraige itself

FAMILY BUSINESS

John Wayne's eldest children recall a life filled with surprising normalcy when he was home, followed by long stretches without him while he traveled the world making movies. Most of Duke's children played small roles in many of his films, but Patrick and Michael, pictured here with their father on the set of *Hondo* (1953), took a special interest in John Wayne's career. Michael helped produce many of his father's films, and Patrick became a professional actor, learning the ropes by co-starring in several pictures with his father. From these letters, it seems Duke also taught Patrick about love, pig latin and keeping up with dear ol' dad.

JOHN WAYNE

October 18, 1977

Dear Pat:

The 'phone lines are still open to the beach. I live here by myself, have five bedrooms. You could come down and stay overnight if it is too inconvenient to drive this far south; or you could pick up the 'phone--either of two numbers and say hello. I know I feel embarrassed when I think about how little I paid attention to my folks, but Christ, it wasn't a year at a time.

Give Michael Ian and Melanie a hug for me and kiss little old "no name" whom I have never seen.

Love,

Dad.

JOHN WAYNE

June 13, 1978

Dear Atpay:

I am glad to hear that you are trying to get control of your lip. It'll do a lot toward insuring a straighter nose.

Of course, you have your father and older brother's magnificent complexion so you have nothing to worry about there.

It's a cinch that everybody in California needs an RK--- pig latin speaking.

Your Dad,

Oink

"Oink" Wayne

Playa Las Gaviotas
Apartado Postal 207

Hotel Playa
MAZATLAN

Teléfonos 44-99 · 55-00
Telex · 066-848

MAZATLAN, SINALOA, MEXICO

Dear Daddy,

Arrived at Mazatlan and it is lovely! I've done a little more shopping and picked up some leather shoes, (that is suede, pinks & whites) for Laura, Marcelita, and Molly.

Met Captain Jack and he invited us to go fishing, Greg went and caught a Saphia - ... Bill fixed dinner and we had Chicken (hooray!) and the fish, it really wasn't as bad as I expected, (hooray)!

I haven't missed an "open market" in any of the cities we've visited (it's a shame I didn't go fishing and avoid the free market of Mazatlan) here you get good bargains like everywhere else and also *free* flea bites! I've had a wonderful time and I wish you could have come to Mazatlan and relax with us!!

Greg and I really enjoyed being in Durango with you and meeting your co-workers.

Thank you for the gorgeous necklace and ring, the jupriel code and remembering that

3

I'm only twenty - two years old —

With much love,
Melinda and Greg.

To My Sweet Daddy

HAPPY BIRTHDAY, DUKE
From left: Birthday wishes to John Wayne from Aissa, Ethan and Marisa. Because the trio were the youngest of Duke's children, they had ample opportunity to spend time with their father, whose work load had lightened substantially compared to the schedule he kept in his younger years; Marisa joins Duke between scenes on the set of *Hellfighters* (1968).

I Love

YOU

X X X X X X
O O O O O O
X X X X X X
O O O O O O

I am sorry that I can't be here on your Birthday. I Love you
Love Aissa, Ethan and Marisa

CATHY

Dear Mr. Wayne:

We went to see your picture "War Wagon" with Mrs. Wayne and Ethan and I thought it was very good. It was really funny when Ethan yelled out "There's my dad" Mrs Wayne has been wonderful to us we have seen some movies at your house and went to look at the Wild Goose.

This is my first fan letter, I just wanted you to know that you are my favorite actor.

Love,

Cathy McDonell

Camellia Motel
Columbus, Ga.
Sept. 18, 1967

Dear Cathy,

Thank you so much for your nice note on
your beautiful stationery.

I am happy that Ethan is proud of his dad,
and am pleased that I have a new fan.

Sincerely,

John Wayne

Miss Cathy McDonell
1010 Sand Piper
Corona Del Mar, Calif.

JOHN WAYNE
WITH WIFE PILAR

"Tomorrow is the most important thing in life. Comes into us at midnight very clean. It's perfect when it arrives, and it puts itself in our hands. It hopes we've learned something from yesterday."

Dear Mr. Wayne,

We enjoyed your performance in True Grit. We hope you receive an Oscar for this movie.

Your fan's always,

Anita La Cava
Anita La Cava

Brigid La Cava
Brigid La Cava

Teresa Wayne
Teresa Wayne

HOP ON POP
John Wayne also relished the affection of more than 20 grandchildren, including Toni's daughters, Anita and Brigid La Cava, Michael's daughter, Teresa Wayne, and Melinda's daughter, Laura Muñoz, pictured here (left) with Duke and his youngest daughter, Marisa (right).

January 14, 1970

Dear Anita, Brigid, and Teresa:

I appreciate very much receiving your poison-pen note.

You're really my favorite fans, because you're part of my heart. I love you all very dearly.

HOLD ON TO YOUR HAT
Duke and Ethan make a splash at California amusement park Knott's Berry Farm. Despite John Wayne's high profile, he was never too busy for quality time or a quick chat with his children. "The most important lesson he taught me was to move forward," Ethan says. "Don't get stuck on little things. Don't get caught up in the petty and the small."

Monday, Feb. 15, 1965

Dear Pilar and Duke:

By the time this reaches you I hope your family is all together again
and comfortably settled. When you have some free time I would like
to hear about the trip from Durango to Mexico City, via motor trailer,
if you finally went that way.

Ken Reafsnyder asked me to pass on to you both the information that
arrangements have been made for a Richfield plane to fly all six of you,
(Waynes, Reafsnyders and Saftigs) to Cabo San Lucas on March 29th.
Ken has made the hotel reservations there, and, according to him after
a few days the men will take off for that fishing expedition.

Al Ybarra went down to Newport last Saturday and is planning to call
you tonight to talk about the house. One of the things he wants are the
plans.

The reason Aissa did not have all of her school books and assignments
to take to Mexico with her is that I did not get the message for her to
travel with Mrs. Martin until Thursday evening, and the following day
was Lincoln's birthday and a school holiday. I did contact Mrs. Strom
at her home, but she said I would have to wait until Tuesday (tomorrow)
for the assignments, as Aissa's teacher would have to make them up.
I am sending down the extra books and the assignments with Cliff and
Betty Lyons, who are leaving Wednesday for a few days' visit in Mexico
City. They will stay at the Alameda, and Cliff said he would get the
books, etc. to you. (If you want, perhaps he can bring back the plans
of the house for Ybarra).

I am also enclosing a new health card for Aissa. The one she took
with her to Mexico expires Feb. 27th and if she returns after that date,
she will need the new one. She was vaccinated last Friday by Dr.
Mitchelson, but we couldn't get a Health Dept. certification because it
was Lincoln's birthday and no county offices were open.

Am also enclosing two Travel Permit letters (in blank, to be filled out
and signed) for Aissa and Ethan, if they have to return to the U.S. with
someone other than you or Duke. These letters can also be used by
either you or Duke in case you have misplaced the previous ones I
prepared in Durango. All of Aissa's papers, her passport, tourist permit,
etc. were in an envelope that she carried with her.

Sally called to invite Aissa and Ethan to Josh's birthday party on Feb. 21st,
and was surprised to learn that they were both with you. She sounded fine,
but didn't have much to say.

Pilar, I never did get back that envelope which the office sent to me in Durango. Did you find out anything about it. I had the Paramount Production Office check with the hotel down there, and they didn't even remember receiving it. It had mail from the office, etc.

Everything here is about the same. Weather nice, but a little on the cool side. I am feeling well again - I foolishly kicked closed a file drawer with my left foot instead of leaning over and doing it the right way, so, of course, I got a pulled muscle in my left knee and leg, and I know better than that. That is my bum knee anyway, and I should be careful about it.

Have spoken with Toni and Melinda and both they and the new babies are fine; and Michael says Gretchen is okay again.

So, if you have time, write. We all send love.

KEEPING UP WITH KIDS

From left: An update on Duke and Pilar's children from one of his secretaries. An avid traveler, Duke frequently brought his children with him on trips for both work and leisure. "He often let me go with him on location," Ethan says. "I might start school, and then, a couple weeks later, he might say, 'Get your stuff and let's go to Mexico.' It wasn't your typical kindergarten through eighth grade experience. But I always learned things"; John Wayne and Pilar show off baby Ethan to his big sister Aissa.

"I hope my family and my friends will be able to say that I was an honest, kind and fairly decent man."

Close As Kin

Although not bonded by blood, Duke considered his secretaries family.

 ARY ST. JOHN SERVED LOYALLY as John Wayne's secretary from the time he was a contract player at Republic Studios in 1946 until her retirement in 1975, when her assistant Pat Stacy took the reigns. In addition to his employees, the women were Duke's dear friends and confidants. While he traveled, St. John, and later Pat Stacy, kept the actor in touch with fans and colleagues, also updating him on family and personal developments. Most often, correspondence was upbeat, warm and personal, particularly when Duke's family was concerned. In one letter, St. John thanked Wayne for sending pictures of daughter Aissa and son Ethan while on vacation, stating, "I could eat them up, they both look so adorable."

WU western union   Telegram

```
      DCA119(1731)(2-092569E334)PD 11/30/73 1731
ICS IPMRNCZ CSP
 2134693510 NL TDRN HOLLYWOOD CA 100 11-30 0531P EST
PMS JOHN WAYNE HOLD FOR ARRIVAL, DLR
CARE PIERRE HOTEL 5 AVE AT 61 ST
NEW YORK NY 10021
WE HEREBY BESTOW UPON YOU THE "GG" AND "BB" AWARD FOR BEING
THE GREATEST GUY AND THE BEST BOSS IN THE WORLD THIS IS A UNIQUE
AWARD AS IT IS THE FIRST TIME IT HAS BEEN BESTOWED UPON ANYONE
AND THE LAST TIME WE THINK THE OTHER AWARD YOU ARE RECEIVING
IS MIGHTY FINE TOO CONGRATULATIONS LOVE
   PAT AND MARY
NNNN
```

The Pierre — NEW YORK

Dear Mary & Pat
Thanks for your thoughtfulness. It came in handy New York clear and sun shiny. Keep this wire for me.
Affectionately
Duke

WORLD'S BEST BOSS

When John Wayne was in New York in 1973 to receive an award, Mary St. John and her assistant and eventual successor, Pat Stacy, sent Duke a good-natured telegram (top), in which they gave him their own "award." They called it the "GG and BB Award, for being the greatest guy and best boss in the world." The actor sent the telegram back with an accompanying handwritten postcard (left) asking the duo to keep the wire for him. Opposite: A letter Duke sent St. John while he was visiting Rome.

GRAND HOTEL

ROMA

Dear Mary —

Short note to say hello and that we are in Rome — Pilar down with tourista.

Wrote both Bebs a note. What is brother Bob talking about with Bö re Panama? Bö advised me of nothing.

How are the weekly meetings progressing? Give our best to every- one and our love to You

Affectionately
Duke

AFFECTIONATELY, DUKE
Whether he was traveling by plane, train or automobile, Duke wrote St. John regularly, even when he didn't have much to say. Regardless of his reason for writing, his messages were always capped with love and affection.

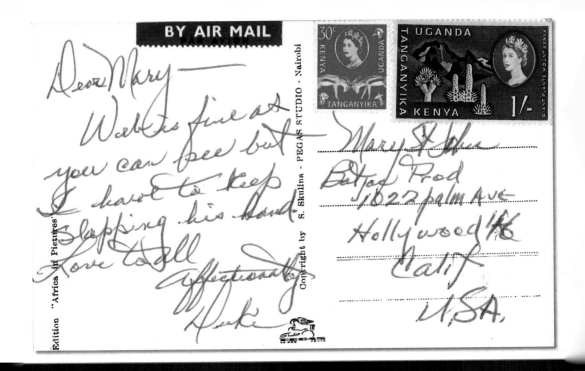

Dear Mary —

Weather is fine as
you can see but
I have to keep
slapping his hand

Love to all

Affectionately

Duke

Edition "Africa in Pictures"

Copyright by S. Skulina - PEGAS STUDIO - Nairobi

Mary St John
Batjac Prod
1022 palm Ave
Hollywood 46
Calif
U.S.A.

Mrs. Mary St. John
Batjac Productions, Panama, Inc.
1022 Palm Avenue
Hollywood, 46.
California.

Dear Mary,

    We are leaving in the morning for the desert. The sun will be
bright there and I will be able to read any mail which arrives and will
be welcome.

    Did Morrison hurt his right hand? Would appreciate at least
an answer to the letter I wrote him.

    Give Pappy my best and tell my tribe to write me.

Love

Duke

Duke

KEEPING IT BRIEF

Clockwise from left: John Wayne with daughter Toni (mentioned in the telegram to right) on her wedding day; given the huge volume of mail that poured into Duke's life from all corners of the world, Mary St. John excelled at a massive job for almost 30 years. And she never hesitated to let her boss know when she was simply too busy for the chitchat the pair enjoyed for decades. She wrote him while he was on the road in 1962: "Send short notes. Do not have time to read long letters"; John Wayne on the road. Instead of a sports car, like most would expect a star of Duke's caliber to drive, the humble actor owned a motor home.

WESTERN UNION TELEGRAM

CLASS OF SERVICE
This is a fast message unless its deferred character is indicated by the proper symbol.

W. P. MARSHALL, PRESIDENT

SYMBOLS
DL=Day Letter
NL=Night Letter
LT=International Letter Telegram

1201

The filing time shown in the date line on domestic telegrams is STANDARD TIME at point of origin. Time of receipt is STANDARD TIME at point of destination

LA116 SSJ469 (02).

L WHA031 (0 CDV154) 82 PD INTL 1/50=NOT FOR HOLLYWOOD
CD ROMATERMINI VIA RCA 9 1935= 1957 MAR 9 PM 5 2
LT MARY ST JOHN=
1022 PALM AVE HOLLYWOOD (CALIF)(BH)=

DEAR MARY ANY WORD FROM YOU KNOW WHO ON THE KRIM
SITUATION STOP THANKS FOR YOUR SUNDAY STINTS AT THE
HOUSE COULD I ASK ONE MORE FAVOR PLEASE FIND OUT WHO
PUT PANEL HEATING IN THE BABY ROOM AND HAVE THEM DO IT
IN THE GUEST ROOM AS SOON AS POSSIBLE WE ARE GOING TO
ASK TONI AND DON TO STAY WITH US UNTIL THEIR HOUSE IS
COMPLETED WE LOVE YOUR LETTERS LOVE=
DUKE=

THE COMPANY WILL APPRECIATE SUGGESTIONS FROM ITS PATRONS CONCERNING ITS SERVICE

"I have tried
to live my life
so that my family
would love
me and my friends
respect me.
The others can do
whatever the hell
they please."

JOHN WAYNE WITH WIFE
PILAR AND SON ETHAN

Letters to
Friends

WORK PALS

Ward Bond and Duke take a break on the set of *The Wings of Eagles* in 1957. Bond shared the gridiron with Duke when they played for USC, and the two remained friends for the rest of their lives.

JOHN WAYNE WITH
FRANK SINATRA

 UCILLE BALL. FRANK SINATRA. GRACE KELLY.
Gene Autry. Elizabeth Taylor. Eddie Fisher.
Joan Crawford. John Wayne's impressive list of
famous friends goes on and on. Regardless of
which part of the globe he traversed or how many
projects he was juggling, Duke was quick to
drop everything to send his closest companions
birthday wishes, congratulatory notes and
plain-old hellos. And they returned in kind. The actor put friends first
and business second, though sometimes the two aspects of his life
overlapped wonderfully, creating cinematic magic and great TV. Among
the actor's closest compatriots were actor Ward Bond and director John
Ford. Whether they were setting each other on fire, playing a hand of
poker or (more often) drinking to one another's success, the ornery
trio's close friendship led to some of the greatest Westerns of all time.

FOR THE LOVE OF LUCY
From left: Duke and Ball on the set of *I Love Lucy*. In the 1955 episode, guest star Duke comes to the quirky redhead's rescue after she gets caught trying to "collect" the cement block with his boot prints from outside Grauman's Chinese Theatre; a letter from John Wayne to Lucille Ball and Desi Arnaz following the actor's appearance on *The Lucy Show*.

5451 Marathon Street
Hollywood, Calif. 90038
January 20, 1967

Dear Lucy and Gary:

I have been in Mexico since September so
missed the "Lucy Show" of which I was a
part. However, many excellent reports
reached me concerning the show and "Old
Duke" -- due as we know to the way I was
carried through the comedy sequences by
Lucy's hard work and Bobby O'Brien's
delightful writing.

It is always such a great pleasure working
with you, Lucy -- you're so dedicated and
so talented.

A Happy New Year to you two and yours,
and my best to all the crew of the "Lucy
Show."

                    Sincerely,

                    John Wayne

Mr. and Mrs. Gary Morton
Desilu Studio
780 No. Gower
Hollywood

JOHN WAYNE AND RED SKELTON AT THE *ISLAND IN THE SKY* (1953) PREMIERE

"I talk to every Tom, Dick and Harry who calls. I certainly would not be too tired to talk to a man whom I consider my best friend—that I have a feeling of blood kinship with."

HIGH PRAISE

A letter of congratulation John Wayne received from Prince Rainier of Monaco and his wife Grace Kelly following his first Oscar win in 1970, along with Duke's grateful response. Before becoming royalty, Kelly was an industry colleague of Duke's, appearing in flicks such as *High Noon* (1952) and *Rear Window* (1954). Although Duke starred in more than 140 films, following his sole Oscar win in 1970, he playfully whispered to presenter Barbra Streisand, "beginner's luck."

```
    WU HD LSA

    WUHD059 JOG                                          APR  9 1970

    LS L CDU325 VX PSX 059 0725 18 PD INTL FR CD MONTECARLO VIA WUI

    APRIL 9 1520

    JOHN WAYNE

    CARE HAL WALLIS PRODUCTIONS PARAMOUNT STUDIO HOLLYWOOD (CALIF)

    HEARTIEST CONGRATULATIONS FOR LONG DESERVED HONOR

        RAINIER AND GRACE              /

    WUT 406P PST APRIL 9 70

    WU HD LSA
```

Ramada Inn
Tucson, Arizona
April 22, 1970

Your Serene Highnesses:

Winning the Oscar was a thrilling
moment to me, but more important
to me are the wonderful messages
of congratulations that I have
received from friends and acquaint-
ances all over the world.

I am most grateful to both of you
for your thoughtful wire.

Respectfully,

John Wayne

Their Serene Highnesses
Prince Rainier and Princess Grace
Principality of Monaco

GAME OF STRATEGY

In addition to his well-documented obsession with the strategy of chess, Duke was also a keen gin rummy and poker player. One of his most famous cowboy scenes from *The Comancheros* (1961) takes place over a card table. The scene features a game of cutthroat poker that ends when Duke's character draws his gun.

Congratulations
by WESTERN UNION

L UDA052 CGN NL PD=TDUD LOS ANGELES CALIF 4=

=JOHN WAYNE=   1966 MAR 4 PM 6 11

2686 BAYSHORE DR NEWPORT BEACH CALIF=

=DEAR DUKE YOU WERE FANTASTIC ON THE SHOW I SAW IT LAST
NIGHT CONGRATULATIONS ON THE WINNING THE PHOTPLAY GOLD
MEDAL AWARD AND ON THE BIRTH OF YOUR NEW BABY MY LOVE TO
YOU AND PILAR=

JOAN CRAWFORD= .

FAMOUS FRIENDS
From left: John Wayne and Joan Crawford in *Reunion in France* (1942). Although the pair only shared the screen once, they remained friends and fans of each other's work for years to come; a note from Crawford congratulating Duke on the birth of his youngest daughter, Marisa, and his Mr. Box Office Award, which he received from *Photoplay* magazine for being the all-time box office champion. On the bottom of the note, Duke's secretary reminds Pilar to reply in kind.

"You can't eat
awards—nor,
more to the point,
drink 'em."

5451 Marathon Street
Hollywood, California   90038

July 9, 1970

Dear Gene:

It was wonderful of you to attend the Headliner
Dinner. I am most appreciative. Frankly I did not
know that it was going to be such an auspicious
occasion. I was overwhelmed at the thoughtfulness
and remembrances of long-time friends.

I'm sorry we didn't get a chance to sit down and lie
a little about old times.

The idea of being your guest for one of the games
sounds terrific. I'll let you know when in the near
future.

Thanks again, and kindest personal regards.

                              Sincerely,

                              John Wayne

Mr. Gene Autry
5858 Sunset Blvd.
Los Angeles, California   90028

A MAN'S BEST FRIEND

From left: A letter John Wayne sent to fellow Western star Gene Autry, pictured here with Duke and his children; John Wayne replies to George Berner, who, among other things, was the owner and publisher of *Dog World*. Duke, who earned the nickname from his beloved childhood dog with the same name, playfully curses Berner after his magazine coaxed the actor's family into purchasing two miniature pinscher dogs.

JOHN WAYNE

9570 Wilshire Blvd., Suite 400
Beverly Hills, California 90212
June 15, 1976

Mr. George Berner
Brae Tarn
Warm Springs, Georgia 31830

Dear George:

They already have a picture of me in most post offices.
I forget what my number is.

When the hell are you going to send me some personal
information about this Carter? I would really appreciate
some critcism and history.

I am sorry I can't make the Hereford Field Day in Georgia,
but I will be pounding the pavements for our picture which
is being released on the 21st of July. I will be in Atlanta
sometime during the first two weeks of July. Will give
you the exact date when I know it. I will be there for two
days for the picture "The Shootist." Boy, I would certainly
like to set me down in Warm Springs in those old slave
quarters I have used before, but it is just impossible.

My love to Bonnie and my sympathies for what she has had to
put up with for so long.

Your everloving,

Duke

John Wayne

P.S. Your damned magazine sold us on the idea of mini-
pinchers. Now we have two, and I can truthfully say that
I have to live in the dog house.

DUKE WITH HIS
MANY AWARDS

"I'm a greedy old man. Life's been good to me, and I want more of it."

1022 Palm Avenue
Hollywood 46, Calif.
April 21, 1961

Dear Liz and Eddie,

I am more happy that you received your
award than if "The Alamo" had received
all that it was nominated for.

Affectionately,

Duke

Mr. and Mrs. Eddie Fisher
Beverly Hills Hotel
Beverly Hills, Calif.

GRACIOUS LOSER

In 1961, *The Alamo* boasted seven Academy Award nominations, while Elizabeth Taylor's performance in *BUtterfield 8* earned her one for best actress. When Taylor won the Oscar, her first, Duke sent congratulations in classic, classy style. *The Alamo*, meanwhile, took home best sound.

To him, reviews and awards couldn't compare to fans and friends. "When people say a John Wayne picture got bad reviews, I always wonder if they know it's a redundant sentence. Hell, I don't care," he once said. "People like my pictures, and that's all that counts."

September 25, 1957

Dear Coach,

Just to let you in on the current news. Bond was on a horse,
and another horse backed into his horse with one of what his
horse had two of at the moment, and cracked a bone in Bond's
hip (?). In that sentence I avoided using that nasty word four
times. They got the shot.

Mary St. John loved the blouse -- Meta's was a little too
small -- Aissa has the dolls right alongside her bed -- and
Patrick Wayne loved the sword. I told him to keep it away
from the tickets.

Herb said you could do the next Vera Hruba, but that you'd
have to come down a little in price, and get Gable.

Bond sends you, through a split bone, what he has piles and
piles of, or am I repeating?

Tuesday or Wednesday I'll be near where the dawn comes
up like thunder.

Ask Michael to jot down, if he remembers, the reference
that you were going to give me of some people in Japan --
and tell him to try Huston some time.

Oh - and the house burned down.

With these kind words, I give you,

Warmest personal regards,

John Wayne

Pen Pals

The decades-long correspondence between John Ford and John Wayne overflowed with humor and affection.

 N 1926, JOHN FORD WAS already among America's greatest directors when he assigned then-Marion Morrison, a USC student working a summer job as a prop assistant at Fox, to herd geese on his set. The director took a liking to Morrison immediately and gave him a few walk-on parts to keep the young actor working until he found the exact right career-launching role. That movie was *Stagecoach* in 1939. Thirteen more collaborations followed, including the 1956 masterpiece *The Searchers*. "Ford took a special liking to me which gradually grew into a very fine manly love," Duke wrote in his unfinished biography.

In the end, John Wayne would describe his relationship with Ford as the closest he'd ever had with another human being. It may not have always seemed that way to the casual observer. While on set, Ford saved some of his nicest words for when the actor was out of earshot—"He'll be the biggest

ON THE JOB
From left: A letter from Duke to Ford. The closeness between the two led Ford to become a regular visitor to John Wayne's house and landed him the role of godfather to Patrick Wayne; Duke takes a break with Ford on the set of *The Horse Soldiers* (1959).

star ever," whispered the director on the set of *Stagecoach*, right after he told Duke that he acted like a poached egg and walked like a hippo. But there was an openness and affection in the duo's correspondence throughout their decades of friendship. John Wayne generally called Ford "Coach" and sometimes "Pappy" or "Jack," and signed off with "your everlovin.'" To Ford, the actor was nearly always Duke.

Even the most casual letters often contained tender moments: "Sure appreciate having your shoulder to lean on" (Duke to Coach) or, "After all, nothing ain't never going to break up our friendship" (Coach to Duke). One telegram from February 1954 read: "Dear Coach: This is an important date in my life because I'm more of a man knowing a fellow who was born on it. Happy Birthday. Duke."

UNSHAKEABLE BOND

From left: Duke, Ford and other celebrities and friends, all of whom constituted the Emerald Bay Yacht Club, a social club, set out to sea; a letter from John Ford to Duke containing some career advice. The note mentions Daniel O'Shea, who in 1955 became president of RKO Pictures. The now-defunct studio made several of Duke's most well-known movies, including *Flying Leathernecks* (1951) and *She Wore a Yellow Ribbon* (1949).

EMERALD BAY YACHT CLUB

December 7, 1955

Dear Duke:

It was nice talking to you the other day.
I certainly appreciate your sentiments
in the matter but I wish you would re-
consider. God knows I want you for the
picture, but you musn't do it as a
sacrifice to yourself. You have been
doing that for me for too many years.
If you have any chance for a great deal
with Danny O'Shea, please be assured
that I understand perfectly. After all,
nothing ain't never going to break up
our friendship.

Incidentally, Duke Kahanamoku was
so pleased when Sam brought him your
message. In fact, Sam said he started
improving right away. He is at Queen's
Hospital and I am sure a short note
would help the old boy.

Mary joins me in love to you and Pilar
and hope to see you after the holidays.

Affection

Coach

Mr. John Wayne
Louise and Rancho
Encino, California

Fort Clark Ranch
Brackettville, Texas
October 1, 1959

Dear Coach,

After I put "Ward" Thompson and guests on
the plane, came back to the Robert E. Lee
Memorial to find you had made an early exit
for the Sunset Limited.

Thank God they went home. I've had a
helluva cold. If you had stayed, I'd have
gone to bed for a night. Am good for about
four hours, then start folding. Well, anyway,
I can make it until Saturday, then I'll sleep
for thirty hours.

Saw the cuts you made on the wall. They
turned out great, as you knew.

There's a light and a camera in the window
waiting for your return. Sure appreciate
having your shoulder to lean on.

Jimmy says hurry back - and "Up The Texans".

Affectionately,

November 4, 1949

Mr. John Ford,
Argosy Productions,
Culver City, Calif.

My Dear Mr. Ford:
   and/or
Bull Feeney:

Due to the fact that you haven't had the experience
of sitting on benches that "Judge" Bond and I have
had, I think you might find these rules very helpful:

(a). You're not allowed to enter the playing field
     without the permission of the coach - Cravath,
     that is.

(b). Inasmuch as there's no camera there, you're not
     supposed to tell the players what to do.

(c). At the end of the game, please leave all
     blankets as you find them. Yours is at home
     in your den, with the ladies' dress forms,
     sewing machines, old drapes, and black and
     tan tams.

(d). If you can get your hands on a helmet and
     noseguard, please bring same for Grant to
     wear at the next bridge game.

(e). The stock company is full. Kindly refrain
     from signing up anyone for stunts or props.

(f). Speaking of stunts, at half-time you will
     hear them call for stunts. Don't be surprised
     when Kennedy, Lyons and Post Parks don't come
     forward. They do it with cards, so you won't
     need Lowell to make a deal with them.

(g). Steponovitch might be in the stands, so look
     out if it's a muddy field.

(h). Please take notice that none of the "kids"
     are playing the game anymore.

LOTS OF LAUGHS
From left: John Wayne gives Coach a quick comedic lesson in the rules of football; Duke and Pappy on the set of *The Alamo* (1960). As an experienced director himself, Ford frequented the set to offer his protégé advice and guidance on the film's direction; an upbeat birthday letter to Coach from his one and only Everlovin'.

January 26th, 1953

Dear Coach,

Congratulations on your 42nd birthday and your good fortune in being able to spend it where you are. It's terribly warm and sunshiny here, but you and I know that's not what I'm referring to.

Also give my congratulations to your opposite number in the field of motion pictures, C O'G. Hope you both have two freshly laid floors - bathed, of course.

And to quote the last few lines of our traditional birthday song:

> We're flat on our ass
> Our room rent is due,
> But never mind about us
> Happy Birthday to you.

Your Everlovin'

BATJAC PRODUCTIONS, INC.

1022 PALM AVENUE

HOLLYWOOD 46, CALIFORNIA

DATE February 6th 1956

INTER-OFFICE MEMORANDUM

SUBJECT Tenant troubles

TO John Wayne

Att:John Wayne -PERSONAL

FROM John Ford

Dear Sir:

As our landlord I am forced to protest to you, especially, considering the exorbitant rates we are paying, about the condition of our toilet. On three separate occasions since we have been here the toilet has refused to flush. I have complained of this on several occasions, but I have been put off...or to use the vernacular..passed the buck...to Webb Overlander, who, they tell me, is in charge of toilets. I am sending you this for your own information.

John Ford

November 4th, 1957

Dear Duke,

Lo. I'm back. Weary. I miss you, but not as much as I miss Web. My hair is down my back. However, it's nice to be back.

I have not seen HIM yet. HE has not called. I don't expect him to.

By now I know you're busy on the picture and I wish both you and Johnny Huston a lot of luck.

Incidentally, I became quite friendly with Kurosawa, the great Japanese director. He is a great admirer of "ours", and would like to have the pleasure of visiting you while you are in Tokyo. He is a terribly, terribly nice guy.

If you see any beautiful Japanese dolls - not babes - dolls - I wish you'd get a couple for Barbara. I owe her several. The last lot went astray. But never mind any samurai swords.

Do you enjoy beer? I do.

Thanks a lot for the books on the Civil War. They're terrific.

Lots of love,

Coach

P.S. Would you like to do a Western sometime?

BEST BUDS

Clockwise from left: John Ford files Duke a good-natured complaint about the condition of the actor's production company bathrooms; Jimmy Stewart, John Ford and John Wayne on the set of *The Man Who Shot Liberty Valance* (1962); another sentimental letter from Coach to Duke. The dynamic duo shared a love of cultural art, beer, Civil War books and each other.

5451 Marathon Street
Hollywood, California 90038
January 9, 1974

Mrs. Mary Ford
74-605 Old Prospector Trail
Palm Desert, California 92260

Dear Mary:

Time, distance, and a busy schedule to keep Uncle Sam happy
and the bureaucracies bulging kept me from seeing you and
Jack as often as I would have liked. And, now, it's San
Francisco, Boston, and London for a Glen Campbell TV show
which I owe him.

Mary, if you should need us for anything, Mary St. John will
be at Paramount. If she is out, Pat Stacy -- who is kind of
taking over for Mary who plans to retire -- and has grown to
love you through our eyes, one of us will always be around.

I hope you get off to a good new year. I figure you read I have got
a few problems of my own.

Many, many thanks for the John Ford western hero portfolio.

Affectionately,

John Wayne

JW/ps

GONE BUT NOT FORGOTTEN

John Wayne was crushed by the 1973 death of his best
friend, but he kept in touch with Coach's wife, Mary,
and daughter, Barbara, for the remainder of his life,
exchanging memories of the man they loved so dearly.

From left: John Wayne pens Pappy's wife shortly
after the director's death; John Wayne and Constance
Towers take direction from Ford on the set of *The Horse
Soldiers* (1959).

"The man was my heart. There was a communion between us that not many men have. I have never been closer to any person in my life than I have been with Jack [John Ford]."

**JOHN WAYNE AND JOHN
FORD ON THE SET OF
THE HORSE SOLDIERS (1959)**

Letters to
Washi

ngton

JOHN WAYNE WITH
RONALD REAGAN

OBODY LOVED AND UNDERSTOOD WHAT MADE America great better than Duke. Freedom. Democracy. Bravery. Hard work. They were qualities John Wayne lived by, and they were qualities he wanted those leading the country to preserve, regardless of which party those leaders belonged to, Democrat or Republican. From his unwavering support of the controversial Panama Canal Treaties in 1977 and 1978 to his praise for champions of the Republican party—Nixon, Ford, Reagan—Duke was outspoken when it came to the policies and the people he believed were best for America. Because, before he was a world-famous celebrity, he was an American. That's how his views were shaped: "not as an actor, but because of my right as a plain American citizen," he wrote in one statement. In these letters to the public and to the politicians who defined the era, Duke's genuine patriotism shines through.

"Respect for the other fellow is what democracy is all about. And I think respect for country goes hand in hand."

JOHN WAYNE WITH
AMERICAN GIs IN VIETNAM

JOHN WAYNE

9570 Wilshire Blvd., Suite 400
Beverly Hills, California 90212
March 7, 1978

Honorable Barry Goldwater
United States Senate
Senate Office Building
Washington, D.C. 20510

Dear Barry:

I was really disappointed that you didn't have the courtesy
to answer me after I made such a point of it to Mrs.
Eisenhower this weekend.

I received a call from Gabriel Lewis the Panamanian
Ambassador saying that the General wanted me to pass on
this information to you privately. He expects to have
trouble with the Communists if this Treaty is not ratified.
He knows that you made no commitment to help, but you had
seemed more sympathetic than your public stance.

I have a hunch that they are going to work on him like they are
on the Somozas. We know that when the Communists start on
the flood tide they hit all over at the same time. We certainly
know what they are doing in Africa. Quite obviously, they
have our State Department saying that the businessmen in
Nicaragua are against the Somozas, but it is strange that the
area in which the revolution starts is up with the Indians and the
uninformed country people around Leon. At any rate, enclosed
is an experience that I had a few years back with Luis Somoza
that might be interesting. The part that might be important at
the moment is that I talked to both sides of the political spectrum,
and nobody wanted the Somozas to leave because they knew the
Communists would take over in 24 hours if they left.

The General told Gabriel Lewis that the Communists are playing
over and over the Reagan-Buckley Debate. Now the Communists
who he is supposed to be in cahoots with are using the Reagan-
Buckley Debate to weaken the General's position if the Treaty is
not ratified.

TREATY TURMOIL

A letter from John Wayne to Sen. Barry Goldwater, in which Duke voices his support for the Panama Canal Treaties, agreements meant to relieve long-standing tension and repair relations between the U.S. and Latin America. The treaties, hot-button issues in 1977 and 1978, narrowly passed the Senate the month after Duke sent his letter, giving Panama eventual control over the canal zone, which the U.S. previously held. Right: Duke pals around with First Lady Mamie Eisenhower at a political dinner in 1959.

Listening to the debate, I am sure it affected you the same as it did me. They were very lovey-dovey, patting each other on the back and belittling the General and his administration and gave credibility to the rumors that the General is a Communist.

At any rate, I guess the General wanted you to have this information without making a public statement. Well, that's about the size of it. That's why I called you.

Sincerely,

John Wayne

JW/ps

P. S. Howard Baker acted like a leader instead of a politician on "Issues and Answers" the other day. Hope you heard it.

P. P. S. I have enclosed some more information on Panama. One, a statement that I made to the Chicago Tribune which they requested, part of which they printed. Secondly, a statement on my recent trip to Panama.

P. P. P. S. If this keeps up, I'll have to register as a foreign lobbyist or something. Man, you should see the letters that I am getting from a special little group in the extreme right. I answer them, and they write me back two more letters. I think they are as bad as the extreme left.

DUKE EXITS A PLANE,
PREPARING TO GREET
THE PUBLIC.

"I've always followed my father's advice: He told me first, to always keep my word and second, to never insult anybody unintentionally. If I insult you, you can be Goddamn sure I intend to. And, third, he told me not to go around looking for trouble."

HOWARD W. CANNON, NEV., CHAIRMAN

WARREN G. MAGNUSON, WASH.   JAMES B. PEARSON, KAN.
RUSSELL B. LONG, LA.   ROBERT P. GRIFFIN, MICH.
ERNEST F. HOLLINGS, S.C.   TED STEVENS, ALASKA
DANIEL K. INOUYE, HAWAII   BARRY GOLDWATER, ARIZ.
ADLAI E. STEVENSON, ILL.   BOB PACKWOOD, OREG.
WENDELL H. FORD, KY.   HARRISON H. SCHMITT, N. MEX.
JOHN A. DURKIN, N.H.   JOHN C. DANFORTH, MO.
EDWARD ZORINSKY, NEBR.
DONALD W. RIEGLE, JR., MICH.

AUBREY L. SARVIS, STAFF DIRECTOR AND CHIEF COUNSEL
EDWIN K. HALL, GENERAL COUNSEL
MALCOLM M. B. STERNETT, MINORITY STAFF DIRECTOR

United States Senate

COMMITTEE ON COMMERCE, SCIENCE,
AND TRANSPORTATION
WASHINGTON, D.C. 20510

March 13, 1978

Mr. John Wayne
9570 Wilshire Boulevard
Suite 400
Beverly Hills, California 90212

Dear Duke:

I don't blame you for feeling disappointed that I seemingly didn't have the courtesy of returning your phone call. When I left the office Friday evening I told Judy that I would be calling her because I thought I had to return to Phoenix that weekend but I wasn't sure and would let her know. However, I didn't speak with her until Monday morning and she told me you had called. We were having bad floods in Arizona and I just had to go out and see what was going on, so I hope you will understand my situation.

Let me make my point again to you, Duke, relative to these Treaties. I would like to be able to approve a Treaty with Panama but this one is so ambiguous, so muddled up that I am afraid if it is approved, it is not going to help Panama, it is not going to help the United States, and five years after the Panamanians take over, in my opinion, we will be back running it or it will be closed.

This is no reflection on Torrijos, it is just a reflection on the instability that Panama has lived through for seventy years. When I was in Panama to observe intelligence matters in my position as Vice Chairman of the Select Committee on Intelligence, I was particularly interested in the communist situation, and while I can't tell you what I learned either in a letter or on the phone, in a general way, I think the communist thing is a bit overdrawn. I would be glad to discuss this with you the next time we see each other eye-to-eye.

Frankly, I didn't hear the Reagan-Buckley debate and, to be perfectly honest with you, I don't think it has had any effect at all on the outcome of the Treaties. I honestly believe that the minds are made up, Duke, and if I were a betting man, I would want some rather good odds if I were to bet that the Treaties would be defeated.

Again, I am terribly sorry about not getting back to you. It was my fault, but let's also include in that blame the good Lord who finally saw it right in allowing rain to fall on Arizona.

I appreciate General Torrijos's attitude toward me. You can assure him that I don't call him a dictator, nor do I paint him in any black way. I think he has the interests of Panama first in his heart, and that is important to all of us. I know just what you are faced with by the far right. They now refer to me as a socialist, so move over.

In hoc

Barry Goldwater

ACROSS PARTY LINES
John Wayne's support for the
Panama Canal Treaties was out
of character for a member of the
Republican party. Like Goldwater,
the majority of the Grand Old
Party opposed the agreements.
Nevertheless, Duke stood firmly
behind his unpopular opinion.

JOHN WAYNE WITH
PRESIDENT GERALD FORD

"This is a good country. With good people in it. Good people don't always agree with one another. Maybe the best thing we can do in this country is agree to disagree every once in awhile."

Dear
Mr. President

John Wayne corresponded with multiple sitting Commanders in Chief.

DESPITE PERIODIC PLEAS THAT he run for office himself, John Wayne repeatedly shrugged at the notion, declaring in a 1967 telegram, "As the saying goes, I'd rather be right than president." While uninterested in occupying it himself, John Wayne wasn't shy about giving advice to whomever held the Oval Office. Duke's presidential correspondence started after he campaigned for President Dwight D. Eisenhower and was invited to speak at Ike's inauguration festivities in 1953. Soon after, John Wayne began corresponding with then-Vice President Richard Nixon, and they eventually struck up a friendship. After Nixon took the White House in 1968, a flurry of correspondence sealed the duo's flourishing bond. At one point, Duke sent Nixon a letter suggesting that the actor would run for president and warned Nixon to "look out." Nixon quickly wrote back, claiming, "Duke is a better title than President!"

John Wayne also sent Democrats JFK, LBJ and Jimmy Carter telegrams after they defeated his preferred Republican candidates, reminding them he was an American first and a partisan second. "Congratulations, sir, from one of the loyal opposition," he wrote to all three Democratic victors. Upon receiving his letter from Duke, Carter invited him to participate in the inauguration festivities, and the screen legend graciously accepted. From that point onward, a curious correspondence developed between the two men, despite their political differences, with Duke periodically sending Carter notes politely criticizing his policies. When the actor passed away in 1979, President Carter eulogized him to the nation, stating, "John Wayne was bigger than life.... He was a symbol of so many of the qualities that make America great." It was a bipartisan vote of approval for Duke's all-American character.

Pres Carter
fec

2-023848E308002 11/03/76 ICS IPMRNCZ CSP LSAB
1 7146469740 MGM TDRN NEWPORT BEACH CA 11-03 1226P EST

► BATJAC PRODUCTIONS PS
9570 WILSHIRE BLVD SUITE 400
BEVERLY HILLS CA 90212

THIS MAILGRAM IS A CONFIRMATION COPY OF THE FOLLOWING MESSAGE:

7146469740 TDRN NEWPORT BEACH CA 8 11-03 1226P EST
PMS PRESIDENT ELECT JIMMY CARTER
100 COLONY SQ
ATLANTA GA 30361
CONGRATULATIONS SIR FROM ONE OF THE LOYAL OPPOSITION
    JOHN WAYNE

12:26 EST

MGMCOMP MGM

PARTISAN BUT PATRIOTIC

From top: Duke's telegram congratulating Jimmy Carter on his victorious campaign for president and Carter's response. Although a devout Republican, Duke always put country ahead of politics and gave the Commander in Chief his due regardless of party.

JIMMY CARTER

November 10, 1976

To John Wayne

Your congratulations are indeed appreciated!

I trust the only area in which we will find ourselves in opposition is that of Party loyalty.
I will need your help in the coming years, and
hope to have your support.

Sincerely,

Jimmy

Jimmy Carter

JC/sc

STATEMENT BY JOHN WAYNE

You are asking that question because of the news impact of a recent
statement in a national magazine. I am going to answer it to the best
of my ability -- not as an actor, but because of my right as a plain
American citizen.

I think the first requisite of our next President is that he be a
God-fearing man -- not necessarily a scholar of deep religious
subjects -- but as in the sense of Abraham Lincoln, who, because
he was not a regular church-goer to any particular denomination, was
once asked his views on religion and if he had ever prayed. He answered:
"Yes. I have been driven to my knees many times by the overwhelming
fact that I had no other place to go."

Secondly, history repeats itself. It has been said a thousand times, but
we seem to overlook it. Franklin Delano Roosevelt, Harry Truman, and
Dwight Eisenhower had the same problems to face that the men in the Alamo,
Houston, Washington, and Lincoln had to face -- perhaps a little more
complex, but basically the same problems. We hope that "The Alamo" will
cue people into realizing that the leaders of that day faced up to their
problems immediately and head-on. They did not complacently sit by and
allow the monster to build for the next generation.

I think the next President should be a man who would emulate General
Sam Houston, who said: "I live by the political axiom of always meeting
issues head-on and at once, rather than leave my children the dread legacy
of their father's indecision."

It is obvious that most of our internal as well as international problems
are caused by one thing: Communism. Not the Russian people or the
Chinese people - but Communism.

Since this is obvious, I want a leader that will confront this issue, even
if it is unpalatable and frightening to the people -- a leader who will make
it uncompromisingly clear that we will fight if that's what the enemy forces
on us; but that come hell or high water, we will not again retreat in front
of Kremlin bullying. If as a nation we do not show some moral guts, we
will lose our strength and purpose as a member of the world community.

My feeling is that our political parties are more interested in votes than
in principle. They are smoke-screening the menace to our very existence
by political generalities and traditional cure-alls, and are avoiding the
main issue. Whether we have more Democrats than Republicans, or vice

versa -- whether Oregon has six-lane highways before Oklahoma does --
is not important at the moment. But whether there is a small footpath
for Communism to the minds of our children is of the utmost importance.
If we are moral and spiritual cowards, they will have no respect for our
way of life.

Therefore, to lead my country I want a man who will take the offensive
against our common enemy -- who will make the people face up to the
possibility of war. I want a man who will raise a banner saying: "Fear
God, but not Communism."

I want a man who will re-establish by thought and deed the United States
of America as a bulwark of freedom and justice -- a man who will make
America's principles and attitude so strong that other Western and Eastern
countries and people all over the world can unite with us to prove the truth
of the latest Chinese proverb: "There can be no peaceful co-existence with
Communism."

The history of the past twenty-five years proves the unpleasant fact that
if a determined unity is not developed in the free world, it will go out of
existence.

I think that the American people are willing and anxious to find a man who
will insure this kind of leadership.

PRESIDENTIAL PREREQUISITES

John Wayne wasn't shy when it came to exercising his
First Amendment right. A practical conservative, Duke
spoke at the 1968 Republican National Convention and
had his own ideas about what made a good politician. In
this statement, Duke outlines the perfect president: a

God-fearing man who, among other characteristics, has
the bandwidth to tackle issues head-on and prioritizes
principles ahead of political parties. One such candidate
who won the actor's support was Ronald Reagan, above
with Duke, Nancy Reagan and actress Gina Lollobrigida.

The Honorable Richard M. Nixon
November 23, 1971
Page 2

You may think me very presumptuous. I hope you do not, but
I would feel negligent in my duty as an American if I did not
make this request as a sincere friend, or at least acquain-
tance -- we have had a martini or two together.

                              Respectfully,

                              John Wayne

JW:ms

219P PDT AUG 1 72 LA288 CTA328

CT JABO55 TC PDF PARIS TENN 1 233P COT

JOHN WAYNE CARE OF MARY ST JOHN SERVICE

5451 MARTHAN ST LOSA

I FOR ONE A CHARTER MEMBER OF THE AMERICAN PARTY WOULD LIKE
FOR YOU TO CONSIDER BEING ELECTED TO THE PRESIDENT OF USA ON
THE AMERICAN PARTY

ELLIOTT E MOODY PARIS TENN.

JOHN WAYNE

August 1, 1972

Dear Mr. President:

Look out!

Watch your Ps and Qs!

BF-1201 (R6-69)

THE WHITE HOUSE

WASHINGTON

August 3, 1972

Dear Duke:

Don't do it. After all Duke is a

better title than President!

Sincerely,

Mr. John Wayne
Suite 332
9071 Wilshire Boulevard
Beverly Hills, California 90211

AUG 14 1972

DUKE AND DICK
Clockwise from left: John
Wayne invites President
Nixon for a drink via the post;
despite encouragement from
fans and fellow patriots, Duke
never ran for president, but
he joked with the nation's
highest in command that he
had the option, as seen in this
light-hearted exchange; Duke
shares a laugh with Nixon.

5451 Marathon Street
Hollywood, Calif. 90038
November 23, 1971

The Honorable Richard M. Nixon
The White House
Washington, D. C.

Dear Mr. President:

Congratulations on your stand on Amchitka.

Quite obviously your time is valuable. I hate to burden you
with anything but, as you know, although I am not a politician
I have taken a firm stand for you because of my confidence
in you as a clear-thinking leader.

Although logic demands some dialogue with Mao, in spite of
200 million victims and a trillion American dollars, and in
spite of much dialogue and bridge building, the attitude of
the Communists has been unswerving; so I'll have to admit
it was quite a shocker when I heard you were going to Red
China and throw Taiwan to the jackals in the United Nations.
Everyone knew that Red China would not accept that seat
unless Taiwan was discarded. All foreign newspapers have
been stating that that was part of Mao's ultimatum for a Com-
munist-Chinese acceptance of a seat in the United Nations.

With all the hysteria about getting the boys out of Vietnam, I
found what I think is a worthwhile article in Reader's Digest,
in explaining to any Doves who would listen, why and how we
were in Vietnam and the reasonableness of same.

So, the favor I would most respectfully request is that in
your spare time you read the Reader's Digest article and
the articles accompanying it. I am sure there are a great
number of Americans who reflect on our government's present attitude as does Mr. Putnam in his article.

You may think me very presumptuous. I hope you do not, but
I would feel negligent in my duty as an American if I did not
make this request as a sincere friend, or at least acquain-
tance -- we have had a martini or two together.

                                    Respectfully,

                                    John Wayne

JW:ms

THE WHITE HOUSE

WASHINGTON

January 13, 1972

Dear Duke:

While this note is belated, I did want to thank
you for your letter of November 23 and its enclosures. Obviously, a very large number of
Americans - myself included - were disturbed
by the expulsion of the Republic of China from
the United Nations. However, let me assure
you that my decision to travel to Peking was in
no way connected with the United Nation's action
as far as this Administration is concerned.

We repeatedly emphasized to every member state
of the UN that the pros and cons regarding the
admission of the People's Republic of China had
absolutely no bearing on the right of Taiwan to
its seat in the General Assembly. We worked
very hard over a long period of time to persuade
the UN members not to expel the Republic of
China. Unfortunately, we just did not have the
votes to win our case, and I think most dispas-
sionate observers of the United Nations share
our feeling that the expulsion of Taiwan only
serves to weaken that world body.

You have pointed out in your letter that logic
demands some dialogue with the People's Republic
of China. I agree, and that is why I am willing to
take the first step. Clearly the generation of peace
we all seek cannot be established while the People's

PIECE OF HIS MIND

John Wayne often sent presidents
articles from magazines and
newspapers that raised salient policy
questions, usually with his own
commentary attached. From left:
A letter in which Duke asks Nixon
about his foreign policy, an area
the president considered his forte;
Nixon's lengthy and thoughtful reply,
underscoring that Duke was more than
able to hold his own with the nation's
highest political authorities.

-2-

Republic is excluded from the mainstream of
world affairs, including contact with the United
States. But we have no intention of abandoning
our commitments to Taiwan, and we have made
this fact well-known to everyone concerned. We
are determined to stand by our friends, just as
we have stood by the South Vietnamese.

I hope this will allay some of your fears and
perhaps clear the air. Needless to say, I always welcome receiving your comments, and
I hope you will feel free in the months ahead to
give me the benefit of your views and counsel.

With warm personal regards,

Sincerely,

ON THE TRAIL
From top: President Ford and Duke share a laugh; the actor's telegram congratulating Ford on winning the Republican nomination for president and the politician's heartfelt response. Duke hit the campaign trail with Ford in Orange County, California, during Ford's unsuccessful 1976 run to retain office.

MAILGRAM SERVICE CENTER
MIDDLETOWN, VA. 22645

western union Mailgram®

UNITED STATES POSTAL SERVICE U.S.MAIL

2-055718E233002 08/20/76 ICS IPMRNCZ CSP LSAB
1 7146469740 MGM TDRN NEWPORT BEACH CA 08-20 0645P EST

BATJAC PRODUCTIONS PS
9570 WILSHIRE BLVD SUITE 400
BEVERLY HILLS CA 90212

THIS MAILGRAM IS A CONFIRMATION COPY OF THE FOLLOWING MESSAGE:

7146469740 TDRN NEWPORT BEACH CA 36 08-20 0645P EST
PMS PRESIDENT GERALD FORD
WHITE HOUSE DC 20500
DEAR MR PRESIDENT MY CONGRATULATIONS ON YOUR VICTORY AND MY
COMPLIMENTS AND RESPECT TO YOU FOR YOUR ACCEPTANCE SPEECH. IT
CLEARLY DILENEATES THE DIFFERENCE IN THE PURPOSE AND POINT OF VIEW
OF OUR 2 POLITICAL PARTIES.
   JOHN WAYNE

18:45 EST

MGMCOMP MGM

THE WHITE HOUSE

WASHINGTON

September 2, 1976

Dear Duke,

It was heartwarming, indeed, to receive your kind and thoughtful message following my nomination. I am particularly pleased to have your generous comments on my speech accepting the nomination of our Party.

In the days ahead we will make very clear to the voters the marked differences in the two major parties. We will do our best to convince the people that the Republican program is best for America.

With warm personal regards and my gratitude for your encouragement,

Sincerely,

Jerry Ford

Mr. John Wayne
2686 Bayshore Drive
Newport Beach, California 92663

P.S. - We want to see you again at the White House. J.

JOHN WAYNE,
THE QUIET MAN (1952)

"You can take everything a man has as long as you leave him his dignity."

UNWAVERING SUPPORT FOR THE TROOPS

In addition to his frequent on-screen portrayals of U.S. servicemen, Duke was an enthusiastic supporter of organizations such as the USO, which helped arrange this visit to Vietnam in 1966. As anti-war sentiment festered at home, John Wayne made it his mission to show American GIs that their work was appreciated. "I can't sing or dance, but I can sure shake a lot of hands," he said.

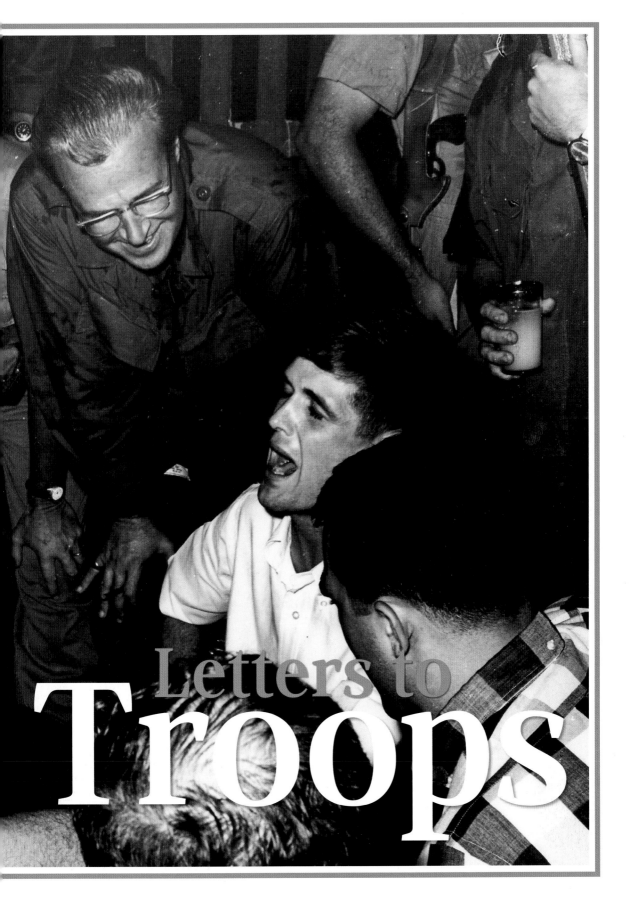

Letters to Troops

JOHN WAYNE
ARRIVES IN
VIETNAM.

UKE DID MORE THAN VOICE HIS SUPPORT FOR THE troops—he proved it on paper. From his stirring portrayals of World War II heroes in cinematic classics such as *Sands of Iwo Jima* (1949) and *Flying Leathernecks* (1951) to his appearance at the Hollywood Canteen to boost GI morale and his tireless advocacy for American troops in Vietnam, John Wayne always backed his beliefs with both his actions and his pen. Paul Keyes, a writer for *Photoplay* who covered the actor's 1966 trip to Vietnam, said Duke savored every opportunity to mingle with the men fighting for freedom on the front lines. "[They] felt his giant hand on their shoulder and a voice saying, 'Hello, Soldier. I'm John Wayne, and I just want you to know that a hell of a lot of folks back home appreciate what you're doing.'" Even after his visit to Vietnam ended, Duke kept in touch with the men he met along the way, taking time out of his busy schedule to send servicemen well-wishes, encouragement and, in some cases, even a little monetary assistance. It's just another example of John Wayne walking the way he talked: like an icon.

"I figure if we're going to send even one man to die, we ought to be in an all-out conflict. If you fight, you fight to win."

No.12, Voie 110 Tuolkork
Mondulkiri Mil. Sub-Div.
Phnom Penh, Khmer Republic
16 June 1973

To Mr. John Wayne:

Sir,

I sincerely hope that you still remember me, but just in case you don't
may be the small souvenir "Bracelet" that I gave you when you visited
Mike Force at Pleiku may help you remember me.

I have a friend named James Morris who is still here with us in Cambodia
told me that he had personally come to your Office and had met your Secretary at that time.

When I was at Fort Benning, Georgia, I've wanted to write you, but I never knew your address though I've tried my best to seek informations. I
have also wanted to write Mr. John Gavin who is my Advisor's (Major German
closest friend. John Gavin also visited our Unit the same year you came,
but that was after your visit. I've seen your film "GREEN BERET" in which
you're the leading man and the mere sight of the Bracelet you wear had
touched me very much. I'm so happy that you seem to value my small gift.

I'm now in exile in Cambodia since April 1967, now a Major in the Cambo-
dian Armed Forces. Next year I'll be sent for Training on Psychological
Operations Course at Fort Bragg then proceed to another Training for the
Command and General Staff Course at Eleven Worth, Kansas. So, with all
the forthcoming trainings before me, I'll surely need your help. Right
now I need three hundred (*300.00) U.S. dollars for my wardrobe and other military uniforms which I couldn't buy because of my meager salary
as a Major. I wish you to know that here in Cambodia all Military Personnel are never issued free uniforms. Also this training though on
Government Status, does not provide us funds for these matters and for
our Pocket Money during the Tour of Training. So this leaves me no other
alternative than to seek the helps of some friends whom I know can help
me. These Trainings are very important for my advancement, that may en-
title me to higher promotions and a higher grade of pay to support my
growing family.

Hoping this letter do reaches you in the peak of health and please do
extend my best regards to your family.

I am.

Very sincerely yours,

Kpa Doh
Major, Infantry

An exchange between John Wayne and a member of the Montagnard, a Vietnamese mountain tribe who fought alongside American special forces. While visiting Vietnam in 1966 to research his movie *The Green Berets* (1968), a group of Montagnards gifted Duke a bracelet to signify friendship. He wore the bracelet during the film and for the remainder of his life. In addition to American soldiers, many Vietnamese recognized the actor and would greet him with eager shouts that he was the "number one cowboy."

5451 Marathon Street
Hollywood, California 90038
August 20, 1973

Major Kpa Doh
No. 12, Voie 110 Tuolkork
Mondulkiri Mil. Sub-Div.
Phnom Penh, Khmer Republic

Dear Major Kpa Doh:

I was pleased to find your address. I will never forget how wonderful the montagnard strike force was to me in Pleiku. I am sure things must be pretty rough for you in Cambodia. Hope the enclosed check will be helpful to you.

Sincerely,

John Wayne

JW/ps

Enclosure: $300 check

HISTORY IN THE MAKING

In December 1965, John Wayne wrote President Johnson to request government permission to make a film about the Special Forces, an endeavor of which the government was supportive. Less than a year later, Duke would tour Vietnam, honoring servicemen and doing research for *The Green Berets* (1968) while visiting the war-torn country.

CONCERN FOR P.O.W. & M.I.A.
NEWPORT BEACH: COMMITEE
VALENTINE LUNCHEON FUND

January 19, 1971.

MR. JOHN WAYNE
2686 BAYSHORE DRIVE
NEWPORT BEACH, CALIFORNIA

Dear Mr. Wayne,

It was not until three days ago that I realized that
there was a possibility that you had not received all correspondence from the CONCERN for P.O.W. and M.I.A. VALENTINE
LUNCHEON Committee. One of our committee members has become
ill and we were not aware that her letters did not get to
you. I would like to apologise for this oversight for myself
and the committee. When Mrs. Blake asked you to be Honorary
Committee Chairman we did not take it upon ourselves to assume
you would take part in the program. Again we thought you had
received a letter asking you if it would be possible for you
to be with us on Monday,February the 8th and if so if you
would introduce the wives and families of prisoners of war,and
honored guests. We also contacted people to ask you if you
would be available,with no result. During this time when we
did not hear from you, we arranged with Dick Richards to sub-
stitute for you in the event that you could not participate in
the Valentine Luncheon Program.
        It is our sincere hope that you will be able to support
our cause with your presense at the luncheon.
        Again we are sorry that we could not get in touch with
you personally. We regret any misunderstanding and hope for
your continued support for the Prisoners of War and Missing
in Action personell.
        I personally would like to thank you for giving your
name to a cause that is so close to me.

Sincerely,

Mrs. Stanley S. Clark
Mrs. Stanley S. Clark

February 8, 1971

Mrs. Carole Hanson
P.O.W./M.I.A. Luncheon
Balboa Bay Club
1221 W. Coast Highway
Newport Beach, California

Dear Ladies,

Our heartfelt sympathies and enthusiastic support to
all in your efforts. Mrs. Hanson, I faithfully wear
the steel wristband with your husband's identification.
Sorry I cannot be with all of you today.

Sincerely,

John Wayne

SENDING HIS SUPPORT

From left: An invitation for John Wayne to attend
a luncheon supporting prisoners of war and those
missing in action from the Vietnam War; although Duke
couldn't attend, he telegrammed his friend Carole
Hanson on the day of the event, sending sympathy
and a reminder that he still wears her husband Capt.
Stephen P. Hanson's POW bracelet.

JOHN WAYNE WITH A U.S.
SERVICEMAN IN VIETNAM

"I can't tell you how proud I am to know each and every man I've met in Vietnam. I wish I could let them know how thankful I am to them for their unswerving dedication."

LIKE FATHER, LIKE SON

om left: A letter from Duke to a serviceman and thank-you note from his veteran father, who the ctor met years before. "I made myself a promise ter I realized I'd really licked the Big C that I'd go to

Vietnam just to shake hands with those kids we'd sent over," John Wayne told biographer Michael Munn. "I did it for their fathers in the last world war, and I'd do i for them because whatever war it is, we all owe a debt to the men who fight for our freedom."

5451 Marathon Street
Hollywood, Calif. 90038
June 5, 1967

L/Cpl. Michael A. Cooper 2264591
H & S Co. AMTRACK PLT.
FPO San Francisco, Calif. 96602

Dear Mike:

I received a letter from your Dad, whom
I met in New Guinea back in his war.

He's mighty proud of you, Corporal, and
rightfully so.

All good wishes.

                          Sincerely,

                          John Wayne

JW:ms

Florence, Ala
June 11, 1967

Dear Mr. Wayne,

I'm sure you didn't expect
an answer, but I'd be less
than grateful if I didn't.

So, please permit this old beat-
up ex-GI the honor & pleasure
of saying thank you, thank you
very much Mr. Wayne. I _know_
that picture will _mean_ _a_ _lot_ to
Mike.

I join you in hoping & praying
that we can avoid the "Big one".

Once again, may the Good Lord
keep you around a long time &
use you to inspire the youth of
our great country.

Respectfully,

Aaron W. Cooper

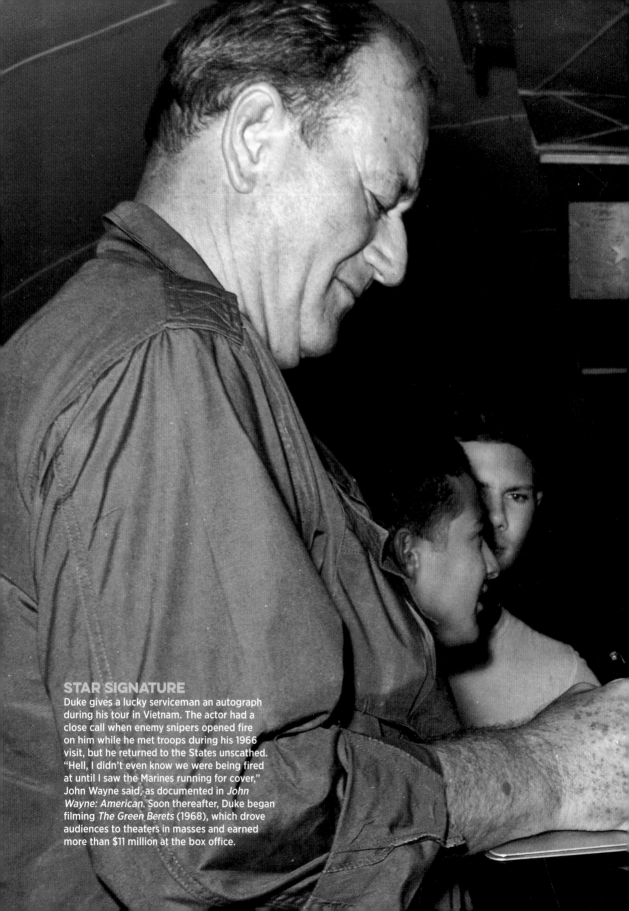

STAR SIGNATURE

Duke gives a lucky serviceman an autograph during his tour in Vietnam. The actor had a close call when enemy snipers opened fire on him while he met troops during his 1966 visit, but he returned to the States unscathed. "Hell, I didn't even know we were being fired at until I saw the Marines running for cover," John Wayne said, as documented in *John Wayne: American*. Soon thereafter, Duke began filming *The Green Berets* (1968), which drove audiences to theaters in masses and earned more than $11 million at the box office.

JOHN WAYNE,
*SANDS OF IWO
JIMA* (1949)

"Give the American people a good cause, and there's nothing they can't lick."

5451 Marathon Street
Hollywood, Calif. 90038
April 18, 1966

The Honorable Arthur Sylvester
Department Of Defense
Washington, D. C.

Dear Mr. Secretary:

This note is to tell you how pleased we were with
the interest and fairness of attitude of all of the
people whom your Department arranged for us
to meet for briefing; and to thank you for your
personal advice in the procedure involving those
groups.

We came away with a feeling that everyone was
willing to cooperate within reasonable limits in
our efforts, and that there is a story to be told
and an image reflected of the dedication and
responsible action of American soldiery in
Vietnam. It is my hope that we will be able to
portray this through our medium within the
bounds of a popular, entertaining picture.

Thank you for your personal attention to our
project, and my sincere thanks to Donald Baruch
for his efficient shepherding of the Wayne group
through the maze of Pentagon protocol.

Warm regards,

John Wayne

JW:ms

Expert Opinion

Retired Capt. Dale A. Dye lists the five best Duke flicks that put audiences on the battlefield.

JOHN WAYNE'S QUIET CONFIDENCE AND SURE STRENGTH embodied that of the American servicemen he so deeply admired, making him Hollywood's go-to candidate for war films. But the sheer number of movies he headlined also makes any comprehensive ranking nearly impossible. "The task is both daunting and greatly dependent on individual taste...in this case mine," Dye says. "And yes, my choices lean heavily to productions where Duke played a Marine. I'm a Marine, and I like films about Marines. Live with it."

MR. DIRECTOR
From left: John Wayne thanks the Assistant Secretary of Defense for guiding *The Green Berets* (1968) crew through the Pentagon. In May 1966, the office wrote, "All of us sincerely hope you will not be out of uniform for long and that the men of the Green Berets soon will have Mr. Box Office as a standard bearer"; director Steven Spielberg and Tom Hanks take advice from Capt. Dale A. Dye, who served as senior military advisor for the critically acclaimed film *Saving Private Ryan* (1998) and also played a small part in the movie as a colonel in the War Department.

CINEMATIC SOLDIER

From left: John Wayne and Robert Ryan act out a scene in *Flying Leathernecks* (1951); Duke in the cockpit in a scene from *The Wings of Eagles* (1957); John Wayne in *She Wore a Yellow Ribbon* (1949).

5. FLYING LEATHERNECKS (1951)

Before Goose and Maverick felt the need for speed in *Top Gun* (1986), this film captured the bravery, heroism and cool factor of Marine aviators. "Duke was likely bringing us his vision of Maj. John Smith USMC, who earned the Medal Of Honor in spectacular aviation feats during the Battle of Guadalcanal in the early days of World War II," Dye says. "And he does a damn fine job of it." One aspect of the military the film gets right is its portrayal of intraservice politics, with the older World War II vets squaring off against the younger, brasher pilots. But no matter where the audience's sympathy lies regarding the aviators' internal squabbles, everyone can agree Duke looks good in the cockpit of a fighter. "It's a treat both for Marines and for people who just understand what cool can be."

4. THE WINGS OF EAGLES (1957)

Duke steps into the role of real-life Navy aviator, Frank W. "Spig" Wead, a visionary paralyzed in an accident and who campaigned for the use of smaller escort carrier groups that would prove a tremendous success in World War II and beyond. "While my taste in military films generally runs to infantry or armor themes,

I'm a patsy for a good aviation tale," Dye says. "*The Wings of Eagles* is one of those that I celebrate as a solid war story." Again, the relationship between Wead and his brother-in-arms, Jughead Carson (Dan Dailey), showcases the best of what military service can foster in those who heed the call of duty.

3. SHE WORE A YELLOW RIBBON (1949)

Not every great John Wayne military movie took place during World War II. *She Wore a Yellow Ribbon* tells the story of an underfunded and underappreciated U.S. Army battling Native American tribes for control of the Southwest. The film's meticulous attention to detail makes it one of Duke's better on-screen efforts in terms of how it conveys to audiences the experience of serving in hostile territory. "The uniforms are just great down to their cut, fit and accoutrements, as are the horse tack and weapons used," Dye says. More importantly, the movie nails the quiet camaraderie that exists between men who routinely put their lives in one another's hands. "The relationship between Capt. Brittles and his loyal, Irish-immigrant veteran Sgt. Quincannon (Victor McLaglen) shows the special bond between two old soldiers—one an officer and the other a senior enlisted man. That's the way it is when it works right—even today."

SILVER SCREEN
SERVICEMAN
From left: Duke and Kirk Douglas
in *In Harm's Way* (1965); John
Wayne gets serious in a scene from
Sands of Iwo Jima (1949). Although
Duke plays a Marine in both of the
aforementioned films, by the end
of his career, he boasted a resume
decorated with roles from every
branch of the Armed Forces.

2. *IN HARM'S WAY* (1965)

The last of Duke's World War II movies
grapples with the doubts and failings of
the members of the Greatest Generation,
which makes their triumph that much
more awe-inspiring. "I especially like the
mission [Capt.] Rock Torrey is assigned by
CincPac [Commander in Chief, U.S. Pacific
Command] to work with the Marines in
taking the critical island of Levu Vana," Dye
says. "It portrays a realistic look at the Navy-
Marine Corps team in the South Pacific
during World War II."

1. *SANDS OF IWO JIMA* (1949)

One of the greatest John Wayne films
regardless of genre, *Sands of Iwo Jima*
features one of Duke's most memorable
performances (it earned him an Academy
Award nomination) that, for Dye, embodies
what it means to be a Marine. "Duke's
rendition of hard-bitten Sgt. John M. Stryker
was pitch-perfect for Marine audiences and for
others who just appreciated the brutal nature
of combat in the Pacific during World War II,"
he says. "The inclusion of real Marine veterans
such as Col. David M. Shoup (who was a hero
on Tarawa and later became Commandant
of the Marine Corps) and three of the actual
second flag-raisers (Rene Gagnon, Ira Hayes
and John Bradley) makes up for most of the
movie's historical hiccups."

"I remember
pleasant and
humorous things,
not the tragedies.
I thank God the
human mind has
little memory
for pain, and
I thank God I have
virtually none
at all."

JOHN WAYNE ON
THE SET OF
EL DORADO (1966)

Letters to
Holly

AMERICA'S COWBOY
In addition to sharing their values, Duke also drew inspiration from the characters he played on-screen, and he even named his youngest son, Ethan, after the character he played in *The Searchers* (1956).

JOHN WAYNE DIRECTING
1960'S *THE ALAMO*

UKE'S FILMOGRAPHY ISN'T BAD FOR A SELF-MADE
man born and bred in the cornfield confines of
Iowa. In fact, it's unsurpassed by almost everyone
in Hollywood, past or present—and likely future.
During his 50-year tenure in what he called the
"picture business," John Wayne appeared in nearly
200 films—in more than 140 of which he played
the lead. "I've been in more uniforms than Georgie
Jessel," he joked in his 1974 NFL foundation speech. "I've been in more
battles than Napoleon and more wars than Germany. I've captured Bataan,
Corregidor, Fort Apache and Maureen O'Hara." But, from a fresh-faced
hopeful who counted himself lucky to be cast as an extra to an A-list actor,
director and producer whose opinion was valued by the brightest minds
in the industry, Duke did more than land an incredible number of roles
on the silver screen. In the process, he earned a spot in the hearts of fans
across the globe and a paramount place in Hollywood history.

JOHN WAYNE AS A PLAYER AT THE
UNIVERSITY OF SOUTHERN CALIFORNIA

"If it hadn't been for football and the fact that I got my leg broke and had to go into the movies to eat, why, who knows?"

NAMES TO BE PUT ON BACK OF MUGS FOR "SONS OF KATIE ELDER"

such as   HAL from DUKE

1.	HAL	25.	RAY	49.	RHYS	
2.	PAUL	26.	WALLY	50.	JOHN	
3.	JACK	27.	FRANK	51.	RODOLFO	
4.	HENRY	28.	ART	52.	STROTHER	
5.	FRANK	29.	CHET	53.	KARL	
6.	CURTIS	30.	DELSON	54.	PERCY	
7.	BILL	31.	DOROTHY	55.	HARVEY	
8.	MICHAEL	32.	LOREN	56.	JERRY	
9.	JIM	33.	WEB	57.	LOREN	
10.	HOWARD	34.	FRANK	58.	RED	
11.	EDDIE	35.	BOB	59.	CHUCK	
12.	ALICE	36.	DEAN	60.	RALPH	
13.	WALTER	37.	MARTHA	61.	JACK	
14.	WARREN	38.	MICHAEL	62.	HENRY	
15.	CLAIRE	39.	EARL	63.	JOE	
16.	LUCIEN	40.	JEREMY	64.	MARY	
17.	DICK	41.	JAMES	65.	AVERY	
18.	DAVE	42.	PAUL	66.	CONNIE	
19.	ART	43.	GEORGE	~~RALPH~~		
20.	STERLING	44.	DENNIS	67.	OLIVE	
21.	TED	45.	SHELDON	68.	MACK	
22.	HAROLD	46.	JOHN	69.	JAY	
23.	GLEN	47.	JOHN	70.	BROWNI	
24.	R.D.	48.	JAMES			

These are for family so do not
put <u>from Duke</u> - just the name

71. DUKE

72. PILAR

73. AISSA

74. ETHAN

*9043 Wheatland
Sun Valley, Calif*

"THE SONS of KATIE ELDER"

MUG CLUB

From left: A list of cast, crew and family members for whom Duke made personalized *The Sons of Katie Elder* (1965) coffee mugs; a mock-up of the image that made its way onto Duke's mugs, which were meant as a token of his appreciation; a letter from Jim Westerfield, an actor in the film, thanking John Wayne for the gift.

Aug 16, 1966

Dear Duke —

I just got back in town and found to my great pleasure the handsome mug which you sent to me.

Yesterday morning I enjoyed my first cup of coffee from it. This A.M., however, I couldn't find it so had to return to my old cup. Later I found your gift on my desk in my den. My good wife has filled it full of pencils, and — to her credit it does look good. Now & then I'll try to sneak it out to the patio & sip some java from it & be reminded of our brief, but pleasant association in old Durango. May God bless you, Duke — you're a good man & a fine American —

Many thanks, Sincerely
Jim Westerfield

HELPING HAND
John Wayne takes cues from John Ford on the set of *Rio Lobo* (1971). Although Duke was a self-made success, he had the director—who over the years became one of his closest friends—to thank for helping him get his start.

"I won't be wronged, I won't be insulted and I won't be laid a hand on. I don't do these things to other people, and I require the same from them."

$\mathcal{F}$EDERATION OF $\mathcal{T}$ELEVISION AND $\mathcal{R}$ADIO $\mathcal{A}$RTISTS

BRANCH OF THE ASSOCIATED ACTORS AND ARTISTES OF AMERICA — AFFILIATED WITH THE AMERICAN FEDERATION OF LABOR

CLAUDE L. McCUE
Executive Secretary

December 28, 1955

Los Angeles Local
6331 Hollywood Boulevard
Hollywood 28, California
HOllywood 4-5125

Mr. John Wayne
1022 Palm Avenue
Hollywood 46, California

Attention: Mary St. John

Dear Mr. Wayne:

I have received the enclosed check from our New York office with the request that we forward it to you. This check in the sum of $25,000 from the Overseas Press Club of America is for your appearance on PRODUCERS SHOWCASE last November 14th.

Would you kindly sign and return, on the self addressed enclosed card, your acknowledgement of receipt of this check.

Sincerely yours,

AMERICAN FEDERATION OF TELEVISION & RADIO ARTISTS
Los Angeles Local

Claude L. McCue
Executive Secretary

CLMcC:s
encl.

cc: Mr. Alex McKee

1022 Palm Ave.
Hollywood 46, Calif.
December 29, 1955

Overseas Press Club of America
35 East 39th Street
New York 16, N. Y.

Gentlemen:

I do not understand the check I received
for $2500.00, which I am herewith returning.

I went on "Dateline 2" as a tribute to, and
for the benefit of, the Overseas Press. If
there is some union ruling that requires me
to take a minimum sum for working on TV -
fine - I will take that; otherwise, please
forget this check.

A Happy New Year, and good luck to your
membership.

Sincerely,

John Wayne

Enc as above

GIVING BACK

John Wayne wasn't one for keeping up appearances—
he was one for keeping his word. After receiving
a generous check in the mail from the American
Federation of Television and Radio Artists for a benefit
appearance he made in 1955, Duke wrote back that he
wasn't sure why he was being paid and returned the
check: His actions were out of charity.

Overseas Press Club of America, Inc.

35 East 39 Street, New York 16, New York. *Phone:* MUrray Hill 6-1630. *Cable:* OPCLUBAM

PRESIDENT: Louis P. Lochner. VICE PRESIDENTS: Kathryn Cravens,
SECRETARY-TREASURER: A. Wilfred May Ansel E. Talbert, Hal Lehrman.

January 12, 1956

Mr. John Wayne
1022 Palm Avenue
Hollywood 46, Calif.

Dear Mr. Wayne:

You were most gracious to return the check for
$2,500 which we had mailed you as your fee for appearing on the
Overseas Press Club "Dateline 2" television program on last
November 14th. The sum was agreed on with AFTRA officials, and
is regarded by them as the minimum fee for the services of a star
of your stature. Possibly anticipating such a generous gesture
on your part, they specifically mentioned they would not want the
check returned.

May I therefore respectfully suggest that you might
consider depositing the check to your account, then, sending us your
own check for the $2,500.

Again, may I express our gratitude to you for your
kindness and generosity.

With our best wishes for a Happy New Year,

Sincerely,

A. Wilfred May

A. Wilfred May
Secretary-Treasurer

AWM/cpl
Encl.

Overseas Press Club of America, Inc.

35 East 39 Street, New York 16, New York. *Phone:* MUrray Hill 6-1630. *Cable:* OPCLUBAM

PRESIDENT: Louis P. Lochner.   VICE PRESIDENTS: Kathryn Cravens,
SECRETARY-TREASURER: A. Wilfred May   Ansel E. Talbert, Hal Lehrman.

February 13, 1956

Mr. Robert D. Weesner
1022 Palm Avenue
Hollywood 46, Calif.

Dear Mr. Weesner:

We are in receipt of your good response, together with return of Mr. John Wayne's check in reply to our letter of January 12th.

This happy conclusion will be reported at the next meeting of the Board of Governors.

Meanwhile, may I convey to Mr. Wayne the deepest gratitude of the Club for his splendid generosity. May we assure you that the monies will be devoted to worthwhile purposes.

Sincerely yours,

A. Wilfred May
Secretary-Treasurer

AWM/cpl

A CUT ABOVE THE REST

Answering his letter from the previous page, when the American Federation of Television and Radio Artists informed Duke it was required to pay a celebrity of his status $2,500, the actor's class shined through: He cashed the check and donated the entirety of the sum back to the federation.

"I want to play a real man in all my films, and I define manhood simply: Men should be tough, fair and courageous, never petty, never looking for a fight, but never backing down from one either."

JOHN WAYNE,
*THE SONS OF
KATIE ELDER* (1965)

Variety

Anniversary like X mas

Happy, I try to look
at people like it was
X mas. Its a kind of
a look of love thy neighbor
a little live and let
live — not trying to
pattern everything into
one mould That kind of
pictures the business the
entertainment world the
industry ~~should~~ have
~~grown up in~~ been raised
grown up in. We are
a little freer than most
~~communities~~ We allow
our children ~~the~~ young
minds in the ~~Industry~~ ~~people~~
a greater freedom ~~let~~ ~~the~~
~~say~~ the insurance field
can allow theirs. As
an art we can bring
into our work the
warmth of a human
being We can reach
the emotions ~~of our~~
viewers with less effort
on their part ~~to~~ less
use of their imagination
than ~~the~~ users of Stone
and paint. This doesn't

Words
of Wisdom

Duke's personal essay reveals the actor's thoughts on the business he loved.

FROM THE FILM INDUSTRY'S first silent pictures to the adventure serials that gripped the nation to the Westerns that would be engraved onto the mythological landscape of America, John Wayne was a comforting constant for audiences and filmmakers alike. Recognizing Duke's elderstatesman status in the industry, *Variety* magazine solicited the actor several times to contribute an essay examining the state of Hollywood. Many stars of Wayne's stature would have immediately handed off the assignment to a publicist. But Duke never made a habit of shirking his responsibilities. He put pen to paper and shared his insight into and predictions for an industry that continues to bring hope and joy to the entire world.

TELLING IT LIKE IT IS From left: A handwritten draft of Duke's essay for *Variety*, in which he calls on his colleagues in Hollywood to make a "positive product" and warns against being "careless and unimaginative"; Duke holds court with the press in Berlin, where he traveled to attend the European premiere of his 1956 film *The Conqueror*.

NO LOOKING BACK

From left: Duke finds himself
surrounded by reporters. Over
the course of his career, he
developed relationships with
some of the entertainment
press's most colorful
personalities, including gossip
columnist Hedda Hopper;
the typed version of John
Wayne's typed essay (right)
about the forward-looking
picture business.

DAILY VARIETY ANNIVERSARY EDITION

Anniversary is like Christmas. Happy. I try to look at people like
it was Christmas. Kind of like "love thy neighbor" - "live and let
live" - not try to pattern everything into one mold.

In the picture business - the entertainment world - the industry in
which I have been raised, grown up in - we are a little freer than
most communities. We allow our children, the young minds in the
industry, a greater freedom and less discipline than say the insurance
field can allow theirs.

As an art, we can bring into our work the warmth of a human being.
We can reach the emotions of our receivers with less effort on their
part, less use of their imagination, than the users of stone and paint.

This does not give us the right to be careless and unimaginative in
molding our results. Our art is a panorama of life - salt and pepper -
good and bad - oil and water - the reasonable and unreasonable
antagonism of human beings.

There is plenty of room and challenge to produce positive product.
Negative thinking - disparaging - belittling - is not productive. It's
easier to degrade, takes less imagination to destroy a feeling of hope
than to build one. So if one would make a quick buck, or become an
over-night controversial personality, the easiest way is to tear down
the images and destroy the hopes and wishes of the audience.

Ours is a forward-looking business - not one of looking back. Too
much in the present and too much in the future - no time to look back.
Except perhaps at anniversaries - then only for the satisfying feeling
of what has been accomplished.

BIG MAN, BIG LAUGHS

John Wayne gives the camera a hearty guffaw. Although Duke often played gruff, no-nonsense characters on the screen, the man himself appreciated a good joke off camera. According to his daughter Marisa, Duke would try to convince her sister Melinda that the London house they lived in during the filming of *McQ* (1974) was haunted. "He'd sneak into the room in the middle of the night to tilt the paintings on the walls and move a jacket from a chair to the floor to mess with her," Marisa remembers.

DUKE BEHIND THE CAMERA
FOR *THE GREEN BERETS* (1968)

"Well, you like each picture for a different reason. But I think my favorite will always be the next one."

Letters to Fans

OHN WAYNE COMMUNICATED WITH HIS
admirers in a coordinated, tactful manner, as befits
a man who remains the embodiment of class and
old-school masculinity decades after the height of
his career. The vast flood of fan mail Duke received
necessitated that he hire a number of secretaries
to work in his home office—sometimes as many
as four at once—to read cards, notes and letters
from his adoring public and craft thoughtful replies in the always on-the-
go actor's place. But Duke also made sure to carve time out of his schedule
to personally respond to as many fans as possible. Be they bright-eyed
Boy Scouts or older, ailing fans, he was never too busy to pen words of
encouragement or advice to the public he credited with his success. The
following exchanges are just a handful of the classic correspondences
between John Wayne and his fans. They showcase the actor's humor,
kindness and wisdom—the same characteristics that made him such a
beloved figure in the first place.

"Why do they like to watch me? I think it's because there's something about the character I play that they identify with. I've been around so long, and I've made so many pictures, some good and some pretty bad, that people have had a chance to see me in all kinds of situations. And each person identifies with the image he or she likes best."

JOHN WAYNE,
HONDO (1953)

July 9, 1973

Mr John Wayne.

Mr Wayne you are the greatest movie star, and there will never be any one greater.

This might a foolish letter too you, but it is the greatest thing I have ever asked for.

I am, a, disabled abled veterand, my wife and I have to leave our home, I will enter into the hospital, and I pray I can come back out but I do not have much of a chance.

I want to have a little farewell get to-gether with my love one's, I can't pay you like the money you get any where you go, I am pretty sure I can pay whot ever it cost you to come, and it will be the greatest thing ever happen, to me why I am writting you, is because I suppose I love you, I have given my life for my country and my people, I have not asked. for much, Asking you to come to this little farewell party is the greatest thing I have ever asked for, for so long you have been the only star too me, you will always be the only one

Mr Wayne I am very much afraid to go to the hospital.

Courage, I know you can give that to me, I have been so scared, Mr Wayne I will pray so hard, and if it would possible for you too come to come to this little party, I would never be scared or afraid any more Mr Wayne I thank you with all my heart.

Mr Walter, L Rogers

Ocean Shores, Washington
July 25, 1973

Mr. Walter L. Rogers
31 Indian Trail
Warren, Ohio 44481

Dear Walter:

I am on location and it will be impossible for me to
come to your party. I suggest you stop calling it a
farewell party. I am sure pain is not new to you.
Go in there and tough it out. Let me know when you
are getting well.

Sincerely,

John Wayne

JW/ps

BEST WISHES

Clockwise from left:
An ailing fan writes
to John Wayne, and
Duke wishes a speedy
recovery in response.
Duke was no stranger to
soldiering on despite ill
health. On April 9, 1979,
the 71-year-old actor
made an appearance at
the Academy Awards
while battling cancer for
the second time; John
Wayne finds a surface
to pen his signature for
a young fan.

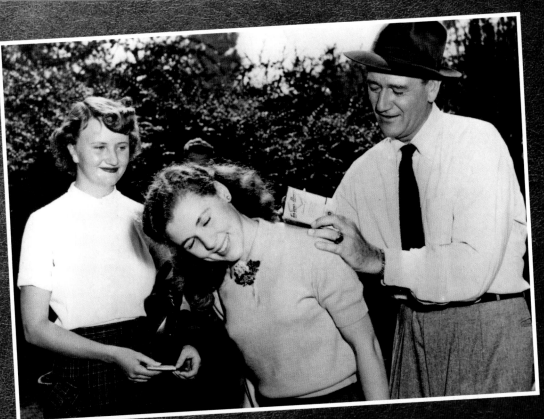

BEAR HUG
From left: John Wayne arrives at the airport in Berlin for the European premiere of *The Conqueror* (1956). He was greeted by a boys choir, a Berliner bear and beauty queens Inge Wax and Gitta Gorzelany; a premade autograph card John Wayne used to save time when greeting fans; Duke poses with a troupe of uniformed tots.

My Father's Favorite Things

Even when he was on top of the world, Duke always remembered those who helped get him there.

T HE MOST FAMOUS ACTOR in the world drove a station wagon. That's the sort of contradiction that defined John Wayne's lifestyle; he was a man who could have anything he wanted, but he avoided the excesses that marred so many celebrity reputations. Instead, Duke was content to live just like anyone else in Newport Beach, California, the small beach town the actor had called home since 1965. "People might call out 'Hey Duke!' when he was running errands, but my father could move about pretty freely," says the actor's son Ethan. "Obviously everybody wanted to talk to him about something, no matter how trivial, but he handled it very well. He had an enormous capacity for kindness toward his fans."

Outside of the idyllic shelter Duke carved out for himself in Newport Beach, throngs of admirers would often descend upon him the moment he was recognized. Like a character from one of his Westerns, John Wayne ventured out into this wilderness prepared, in this case armed with a stack of autographs instead of firearms. "He had autographed cards

NURTURING THE FUTURE
John Wayne, pictured here with a group of young, athletic fans, made his fame playing cowboys of the past, but he always kept an eye pointed toward the future. He often lent his fame to organizations he knew would help mold America's youth into upstanding citizens, such as the Boy Scouts of America and Little League Baseball.

HARD AT WORK

Whether traveling to England, Japan or one of the many states in the union, John Wayne always made time to interact with the people who kept him employed as an actor: his audience. Duke's desire to bring quality films to a paying public also led him to direct and produce. He ran several production companies including John Wayne Productions, Wayne-Fellows Productions and Batjac Productions.

"[My father] was someone who came from humble beginnings."

made up and would hand them to fans so he could make it through the crowd," Ethan says. The actor felt obligated to give back to those who had made him a success, even if the overwhelming demand he faced limited his gifts to a simple autograph. "He was someone who came from humble beginnings and spent years in the trenches of Hollywood working on B-movies," Ethan says. "He understood the fans allowed him to live his life and do his work, and he was forever grateful to them."

Beyond autographs, John Wayne showed his appreciation for his audience by tirelessly answering as much of his fan mail as he could. "He received an inordinate amount of mail," Ethan says of the sacks of correspondence that would arrive at the house every day. Duke had three full-time secretaries come to the house daily at 9 in the morning and they'd stay until 5 in the afternoon to help the actor sort through the hundreds of well-wishes, questions about his movies and requests for aid sent his way. "Mary St. John led the secretaries in reading out all the letters to him and getting his responses," Ethan says.

MAN OF MANY HATS

John Wayne signs autographs for his little league team, the Giants. Duke sponsored and coached the team, teaching L.A. boys about sportsmanship and the great American pastime.

But sometimes fans pushed the limits of even Duke's tolerance. Ethan recalls some of John Wayne's less ethical admirers talking their way into the actor's living room by claiming to be members of the press. "He would take the time to answer the door and spend five minutes with them, only to find out it was all a hoax so they could get close to John Wayne," says Ethan. But not all uninvited visitors were unwelcome. "One night when I was around 10, we heard a noise down by the dock next to our house, and my father went down there with his gun to check it out," says Ethan. "It ended up being some soldiers who had just returned from overseas." The servicemen had rowed over to Duke's house, but at the last minute decided disturbing the legendary toughman in the middle of the night might not be the best idea and were debating leaving. "He told them, 'Come on up and have a drink with me,' and they talked for about a half hour before Dad sent them on their way." A typical tale of an atypical man.

JOHN WAYNE,
*RIDERS OF
DESTINY* (1933)

"Courage is being
scared to death but
saddling up anyway."

CITY OF LOS ANGELES
CALIFORNIA

OFFICE OF THE
CHIEF OF POLICE
EDWARD M. DAVIS

SAM YORTY
MAYOR

DEPARTMENT OF
POLICE
150 N. LOS ANGELES ST.
LOS ANGELES, CALIF. 90012
PHONE: 624-5211

IN REPLYING PLEASE GIVE
OUR REF. NO.

December 11, 1969

Dear Mr. Wayne,

We the members of the graduating class of 8-69, cordially invite you, as our special guest, to attend graduation exercises to be held at the Los Angeles Police Academy on December 26, 1969, at 1:00 P.M.

The graduating class of 8-69 is unique in that we are the first class of recruits that has both men and women in training together. All classes in the Academy are co-educational, with the men and women equally participating in all phases of the physical training. To illustrate a point, our physical training instructor would use you to emphasize the qualities he wanted to see in us. When we were ready to quit, someone would yell out, "John Wayne's my hero" and it would give us that added incentive to try a little harder.

Graduation day will be a special day for us and we would consider it an honor to have you present at the ceremony, as you have been an inspiration to all of us.

CLASS OF 8-69
LOS ANGELES POLICE DEPARTMENT

Enclosures

R.S.V.P. Mrs. Karen Fleming, Class Secretary
1072 Appleton Road
Simi, California 93065
805 527-7597

5451 Marathon Street
Hollywood, Calif. 90038
December 29, 1969

Dear Gals Of The Graduating Class of 8-69:

I can't tell you how disappointed I am that I could not
attend your graduation exercises. I had promised to
take my family to Aspen for Christmas, so was not
here to accept your invitation.

That's a mighty dangerous looking group in that photo,
and I'm certainly going to try to continue to keep
policemen as my friends.

Seriously, my compliments and congratulations to
you ladies. As a citizen, I'm very proud of you.

Sincerely,

John Wayne

Class Of 8-69
Los Angeles Police Department
c/o Mrs. Karen Fleming
1072 Appleton Road
Simi, Calif. 93065

March 10,1973
S.I.,N.Y. 10302

Dear John,

   I finally finished your afgan, it usually
takes me 5,6and 7 months to make one, this
one I finished in a little over a month. Of
course I worked on it every chance I could.
Some people have tried to pay me to make these
but I wont take money because I just make them
for relatives and special ones, I dont think
there could be any better present like one
made. This has 86685 stitches in it and all
just for you. These are good and warm, I hope
you like it and use it. I made it a little
extra long because you are so tall. Please
just let me know you received it.
   Take care and remember we love you.

                    Sincerely,
                    Sophie Marsac
                    Your 36 (going on 37)year fan
                    Mrs Sophie Marsac
                    37 Jewett Ave.
                    Staten Island, New York 10302

5451 Marathon Street
Hollywood, California 90038
March 27, 1973

Mrs. Sophie Marsac
37 Jewett Avenue
Staten Island, New York 10302

Dear Mrs. Marsac:

Thank you so much for the beautiful red, white,
and blue afgan. I can assure you that it will be
used, and I appreciate all the work you put into
it.

Sincerely,

John Wayne

JW/ps

CLASSIC STYLE

Much of John Wayne's iconic wardrobe came in the mail, but not just in the form of afghans from fans, as mentioned in the exchange to the left. Duke used catalogs from companies such as Eddie Bauer to order the majority of his clothing. In doing so, he could avoid being mauled by fans at the local mall; Below: One such fan greets John Wayne with flowers as the star steps out to enjoy a cup of joe.

Mr. James M. Downey

President, Harvard Lampoon

I accept with pleasure your challenge to bring my new motion
picture MCQ into the pseudo-intellectual swamps of Harvard
Square.

Age, breeding and political philosophy aside, I am quite
prepared to meet nose-to-nose and fact-to-fact any or all
of the knee-jerk liberals who foul your campus.

Your intellectual pretensions, your pointy-headed radicalism
your Mao Tse-Tung quotations and your high-school French
proverbs could hardly pierce the hide of a man who has stormed
the Alamo, raised the flag at Iwo Jima and fought with the
Green Berets.

So comb out your beards, extinguish your pot and put a book-
marker in your Marcuse and Hesse....I'll be there on Jan. 15
for the premiere of MCQ, ready to flex muscles with the limpest
bunch of baby-brained scholars in America.

                          Sincrely,

                          JOHN WAYNE

Visiting Hostile Territory

A satirical tradition, a gutsy challenge and an invite Harvard never thought Duke would accept.

CCORDING TO the *Reading Eagle*, on February 24, 1974, "The confrontation was set for January 15, at the [*Harvard*] *Lampoon*'s 44 Bow St. headquarters; the time: High Noon." Though Duke's calcified conservatism was legendary, he had agreed to debate Harvard's anti-Vietnam students who, according to a 2003 *New York Post* article by Phil Mushnick—an eyewitness to Duke's Harvard appearance—had turned the actor into "at least as much as Richard Nixon... the symbol of dim-witted and intolerant Americanism."

But the actor proved anything but thin-skinned or dim. Duke fielded questions ranging from the political ("Do you look at yourself as the fulfillment of the American Dream?") to the absurd (one student asked him if Richard Nixon would play John Wayne in the story of his life). He answered the first question with a self-deprecating quip, "I don't look at myself any more than I have to," and when a student asked about the actor's toupée he rejoined, "This is real hair! It's not mine, but it's real." The visit didn't change Duke's or the students' political views, but they discovered common ground in appreciating a good laugh.

CHARGE!
From left: The actor's response to *The Harvard Lampoon*'s invitation; Duke made his way to Harvard Square Theater in an armored personnel carrier. After the event, photographer Ethan Boatner from the Harvard University News Office found himself face-to-face with Duke. "I asked him how he was, and he smiled and said, 'tired,'" Boatner recalls.

"Don't pick a fight, but if you find yourself in one, I suggest you make damn sure you win."

Walter A. DeMilly

1305 DILLARD
TALLAHASSEE, FLORIDA

January 26, 1967

Mr. John Wayne
Hollywood, California

Dear Mr. Wayne:

A thirteen year old Boy Scout has asked me to
present him his Eagle Badge at a Court of Honor
to be held in late February. You can help me
make an unusual presentation.

My comments for the ceremony will be taken from
the Scout Law. As a former Boy Scout, I am
sure you are familiar with each of its twelve
points.

Your opinion as to which is the most important
point would impress this fine Scout and his
friends profoundly. I shall be forever grateful for your reply.

The letter you write will be given to our young
friend for his Eagle scrapbook!

Sincerely,

WALTER A. DeMILLY

WAD:ac

BRAVERY AND REVERENCE

John Wayne and a group of Boy Scouts practice their patriotism with flag folding. John Wayne always took time to send his regards to the scouts, from congratulatory letters to those filled with his two cents on scout law (as seen at right), which says Boy Scouts are trustworthy, loyal, helpful, friendly, courteous, kind, obedient, cheerful, thrifty, brave, clean and reverent. In a congratulatory 1974 letter to a lucky Eagle Scout, Duke wrote: "I am sure your excellent work and dedication in scouting will bring you great happiness and gratification in knowing that you are helping others."

5451 Marathon Street
Hollywood, California
February 15, 1967

Mr. Walter A. DeMilly
1305 Dillard
Tallahassee, Florida

Dear Mr. DeMilly:

It is difficult for me to separate the twelve points of the Scout Law, but If I were to do this I would say:

A Scout is Brave - a Scout is Reverent. He has the courage to face danger in spite of fear, and to stand up for the right against the coaxings of friends or the jeers or threats of enemies, and defeat does not down him. He is reverent toward God. He is faithful in his religious duties and respects the convictions of others in matters of custom and religion.

Sincerely,

John Wayne

JW:ms

JOHN WAYNE
ON THE SET OF
BIG JAKE (1971)

"I'm an American actor. I work with my clothes on. I have to. Riding a horse can be pretty tough on your legs and elsewheres."

5451 Marathon Street
Hollywood, Calif. 90038
January 4, 1967

Miss Candy Dudley, Feature Editor
The Reverie
4425 38th Avenue
Meridian, Miss.

Dear Miss Dudley:

In connection with the contest you are conducting for
your school annual, my selections are as follows:

Cathy McDonnell - for most beautiful, as well as
                    for Senior Class

Janet Alexander - for Junior Class

Connie Bullock - for Sophomore Class

David Bailey is my choice of the three men submitted.

It is my earnest hope that those young ladies and men
not chosen will not be too disappointed. It is most
difficult to make selections from photographs, as they
do not always reflect the true beauty, handsomeness or
character of the subject.

All good wishes to The Reverie and to the students of
Meridian High.

                              Sincerely,

                              John Wayne

JW:ms

A THORN AMONG ROSES

From left: John Wayne acts as a judge for a high school beauty contest via the post; Duke finds himself surrounded by a bevy of beauties drawn to the actor's charisma. Though much admired by women, John Wayne proved himself to be a devoted family man, even going so far as to help pick out dresses for wife Pilar when the pair went shopping together.

Get Well Soon

John Wayne didn't battle the Big C alone—legions of fans stood firmly behind the silver screen hero.

EVEN FOLLOWING HIS 1964 lung cancer diagnosis, Duke continued to extend every effort to connect with the people who helped make him a success. Like always, letters addressed to the actor poured in, but they were more than just regular fan mail. In these batches, fans took their turns inspiring the actor who had so many times lifted their spirits, be it with a donation to the American Cancer Society in Duke's name, a hand-drawn illustration or a simple get-well card filled with wishes for a quick recovery.

A Gift in Your Honor

Mr. John Wayne

CONQUERING CANCER

George Berner, a personal friend of John Wayne's, was one of many to donate to the American Cancer Society in the actor's name. After his diagnosis, Duke worked with the organization to advise Americans to keep tabs on their health. "Get a checkup. Talk someone you like into getting a checkup. Nag someone you love into getting a checkup," he urged in an ad. "And while you're at it, send a check to the American Cancer Society. It's great to be alive."

With this Message...

A speedy recovery

has been received by

The American Cancer Society

from

George Burns

You may be sure that this thoughtful tribute to you will be invested immediately in the fight to conquer cancer. To the good wishes of the donor, we add ours.

1040 North Las Palmas Ave
Hollywood, Ca 90038

August 28th, 1975 —

Dear Mr. Wayne:

I am sorry to hear that you are still under the weather, and I would like to offer my best wishes for a speedy return to good health and activity. In an effort to "cheer" you up (although I'm sure all those cute nurses are seeing to that ☺), I made up the enclosed "CARD".

It's not exactly a Norman Rockwell or a Herschfield, but I thought I would lend my hand at doing an "un-official John Wayne Portrait." This now makes you one of a priviledged handful who own an original MOLONY. ☺

Seriously, I hope you like it, and that it gives you a smile. That is why I did it. I've enjoyed your artistry on the silver screen, so I thought I would share a little of mine with you, limited as it may be.

Please take care of yourself, listen to your doctors (and cute nurses) and again, my best wishes for a quick return to action. We hate to see a good man down —

Your friend & number one fan!

Mike Molony

MOLONY '75

TRUE GRIT

An exchange between Duke and a fan, who illustrated John Wayne as Rooster Cogburn in *True Grit* (1969) in hopes of lifting the actor's spirits. Duke was as fond of the drawings as he was of the screenplay. After seeing the film, he wrote screenwriter Marguerite Roberts to compliment her work. "It was magnificent," he praised. "I thank you for your integrity concerning Mr. Portis's book, and for the wonderful ending you devised in his style."

9570 Wilshire Blvd., Suite 400
Beverly Hills, California 90212
September 8, 1975

Mr. Michael J. Molony
160 1/2 Argonne Avenue
Long Beach, California 90803

Dear Michael:

I want to thank you for your thoughtfulness.
The get-well card you made for me was certainly
appreciated. I can't tell you how much it
means to me to be thought of by people such as
yourself.

Again, my thanks and my best wishes to you for
a full, happy life.

Sincerely,

John Wayne

JW/ps

HAPPY HOLIDAYS

An Easter exchange between John Wayne and an
artistic young fan. Duke loved the holidays, specifically
Christmas, because they brought his family and friends
together. "We'd have the big Christmas dinner with
turkey and stuffing," Ethan says. "Some of his close
friends and family would come by the house, and then
the guys would have fun."

```
                    9570 Wilshire Boulevard
                    Suite 400
                    Beverly Hills, California   90212
                    March 10, 1975



        Deanne Littles
        2238 Arlington
        Long Beach, California    90810

        Dear Deanne:

        You sent me a sweet reminder
        that Easter is near and I
        thank you.

        You have artistic talents to be proud
        of.

        I appreciate you thinking of me
        and wish you the best.

                    Sincerely,



                    John Wayne
```

JOHN WAYNE ON THE SET
OF *EL DORADO* (1966)

"Let's say I hope that I appeal to the more carefree times in a person's life than to his reasoning adulthood. I'd just like to be an image that reminds someone of joy rather than of the problems of the world."

p6: Courtesy Annette Poizner; p56: Moviestore Collection/Alamy; p77: The Mirisch Corporation/Ronald Grant Archive/Alamy; p80: Everett Collection/Alamy; p86: U.S. National Archives; p91: Everett Collection/Alamy; p159: Daily Mail/Rex/Alamy; p189: Courtesy E.B. Boatner; p206: Trinity Mirror/Mirrorpix/Alamy

Topix Media Lab would like to thank John Wayne Enterprises, custodian of the John Wayne Archives, for providing unfettered access to their private and personal collection. Best efforts were made by Topix Media Lab to find and credit the photographers. Topix Media Lab makes no specific claim of ownership of images contained in this publication and is claiming no specific copyright to images used.

Media Lab Books
For inquiries, call 646-838-6637

Copyright 2015 Topix Media Lab

Published by Topix Media Lab
14 Wall Street, Suite 4B
New York, NY 10005

ISBN-10: 1-942556-19-5
ISBN-13: 978-1-942556-19-0

JOHN WAYNE ENTERPRISES

JOHN WAYNE DAILY SCHEDULE - JANUARY THROUGH DECEMBER 1977

Jan. 1 JW in Newport Beach. Cocktails and dinner at home for the De Francos, Gordeans, Reafsnyders, PS, Peggy Reagan and JW children.

Jan. 2 JW in Newport Beach.

Jan. 3 JW meeting in Newport with Clark Powell and Paul Lasarus. JW appointment with Dr. Davis.

Jan. 4 JW in Newport Beach. Appointment with Dr. Hart and Dr. Jones.

Jan. 5 JW and Clark Powell to see Alex Madonna in San Luis Obispo via Madonna's private plane.

Jan. 6 JW interview with Milt Richmond of UPI re: The Super Bowl. Appointment with Dr. Jones. JW interviewed by M. Seneon and Debbi Dovitch of the World Affairs Council. JW telephone interview with Bill Overend of the L. A. Times re: an article on cowboys and cattle.

Jan. 7 JW appointment with Dr. Davis. JW and PS to Pasadena via Barney to the Pasadena Hilton.

Jan. 8 JW in Pasadena to present the Most Valuable Player Award for CBS "Super Night at the Super Bowl. "

Jan. 9 JW to cocktail party for Clark Powell and 10 Houston Bankers at his home in Newport Beach.

Jan. 10 JW in Newport Beach.

Jan. 11 JW in Newport Beach.

Jan. 12 JW and PS attended a cocktail party for Leon Uris at Chasen's.

Jan. 13 JW in Newport Beach. Appointment with Dr. Doan and Dr. Hart. Marisa Wayne had an interview with Jane Ardmore in Newport Beach.

Jan. 14 JW in Newport Beach. Brad Gates and Ernie Saftig for cocktails. Cocktails and movies for the Iversons and the De Francos.

Jan. 15 JW in Newport Beach meeting with Clark Powell and his NRG group.

Jan. 16 JW in Newport Beach. Dinner at his home for 15 people.

Jan. 17 JW, PS, and Barney to Washington D. C. via United Airlines. Stayed at the Mayflower Hotel.

Jan. 18 JW in Washington D. C. for the rehearsal of the Inaugural Concert at the Kennedy Opera House.

Jan. 19 JW working in Washington D. C. complete run through. Joe De Franco came from New York - Lunch with JW. JW & guests had hors d'oeuvres and caviar and dinner in his suite.

Jan. 20 JW and PS to St. Croix via American Airlines. Stayed at Mr. Charles and Maureen (O'Hara) Blair's home. Dinner there.

Jan. 21 JW in the Virgin Islands at the Blairs.

Jan. 22 JW in the Virgin Islands at the Blairs. Dinner at a restaurant Commanche. JW took 10 people to dinner with Antilles Air Boats.

Jan. 23 JW toured the Virgin Islands by plane. Lunch at Rockeresort on St. John Island. Dinner at the Blairs.

Jan. 24 JW in the Virgin Islands. Went shopping. Went to a birthday party for one of the sons of one of the pilots at Antilles Air Boats.

Jan. 25 JW in the Virgin Islands. Visited "Dr. Moreau" movie set with Burt Lancaster. JW & Charlie Blair went flying in Big Sea Plane.

Jan. 26 JW in St. Croix - Virgin Islands. Went shopping. Dinner with Captain Lincoln and his wife Dolly.

Jan. 27 JW in St. Croix.

Jan. 28 "   "   "

Jan. 29 "   "   "   Went fishing with Jack and Dolly Lincoln.

Jan. 30 "   "   "

Jan. 31 JW in St. Marteen with the Blairs via Sandingham - Lunch at La Colanda.